Strategic Intelligence

Strategic Intelligence

Conceptual Tools for Leading Change

Michael Maccoby

OXFORD
UNIVERSITY PRESS

OXFORD
UNIVERSITY PRESS

Great Clarendon Street, Oxford, OX2 6DP,
United Kingdom

Oxford University Press is a department of the University of Oxford.
It furthers the University's objective of excellence in research, scholarship,
and education by publishing worldwide. Oxford is a registered trade mark of
Oxford University Press in the UK and in certain other countries

First Edition published in 2015

Impression: 1

Published in the United States of America by Oxford University Press
198 Madison Avenue, New York, NY 10016, United States of America

British Library Cataloguing in Publication Data
Data available

Library of Congress Control Number: 2014956039

ISBN 978–0–19–968238–6

Printed in Great Britain by
CPI Group (UK) Ltd, Croydon, CR0 4YY

Acknowledgments

In July 2012, I sat down with David Musson at Oxford University Press, and discussed the idea of a book about what I've learned from great thinkers of organization change. David encouraged me to write a proposal that he then sent to three anonymous reviewers, all of whom supported the project. Rafael Ramirez, Charles Heckscher, and Berth Jönsson also read the proposal and encouraged me to develop it. They and the reviewers suggested I integrate what I've learned from these thinkers with my experiences with organization change.

This book also includes work I've done with Tim Scudder and Cliff and Jane Norman. I am grateful to them and to Heckscher and Jönsson, who read drafts of the chapters and made many helpful suggestions. Thanks to Judith Spitz for her careful reading of the manuscript and incisive comments. Others who reviewed chapters and sent helpful comments were Samuel Carnegie Calian, Stuart Holliday, Annie Maccoby-Berglof, Salvatore R. Maddi, Tony Silard, and Doug Wilson. Thanks also to Jon Clifton, who sent me the Gallup studies on employee engagement.

Sandylee Maccoby was also helpful and encouraging. She read the draft chapters and made suggestions that clarified the wording and my thinking.

Katie Berglöf, my granddaughter who is reading philosophy at the University of Edinburgh, suggested the title of the book. She said, "Everyone will want to develop strategic intelligence." I hope she is at least partly right.

After I presented him with the draft manuscript, David Musson proposed edits and additions that I think have improved the book.

Thanks to Maria Stroffolino, who has again been extremely helpful in preparing the manuscript through its many drafts, and making sure that we are following the publisher's guidelines. Both Maria and I thank Clare Kennedy, Mohana Annamalai, and Fiona Barry for helping us get the manuscript ready for production.

Michael Maccoby

Washington, DC
26 April 2015

Preface

Everything changes and nothing remains still ... and ... you cannot step twice in the same stream.

Heraclitus (quoted in Plato's *Cratylus*, 402, a, line 8)

"The best way to protect your future is to create it."

Abraham Lincoln

To make the frozen circumstances dance,
you must sing to them their own melody.

Karl Marx, *Toward the Critique of Hegel's Philosophy of Law*

As Heraclitus observed 2,500 years ago, change is constant. We are all affected by the changing weather, natural disasters, and the march of time. Changes caused by human activity—inventions, migrations, wars, government policies, new markets, and new values—affect organizations as well as individuals. Threats and opportunities call for change. But how organizations change depends on leaders, their knowledge, and philosophy. They can direct change just to improve the bottom line, or they can also change organizations to improve the wellbeing of customers, collaborators, and communities. To create a better future for an organization, leaders need to be strategic thinkers.

As Lincoln understood, the best way to protect your future is to create it. He was a brilliant strategist who foresaw the coming of the industrial age and supported railways and land grant colleges to help create his country's future. He demonstrated qualities essential for strategic leaders: foresight, vision, ability to partner with strong colleagues and to inspire people.

I have worked with leaders in the Americas, Europe, Asia, Africa, and the Middle East for over half a century to change organizations, to improve their results, the quality of their products and services, and the working life of their employees.

This book is based on my experiences and what I learned from great thinkers. It is written for leaders, consultants, and coaches who are working to change organizations to improve the wellbeing of customers, collaborators, and communities. It provides a guide to developing *Strategic Intelligence*:

the qualities of mind and heart that equip leaders with the conceptual tools that:

- prepare leadership teams to change their organization;
- add value for customers; and
- engage, even inspire, their collaborators.

These conceptual tools are like instruments with which leaders can play the melodies that make people dance together in new ways (see Chapter 2).

Unlike many academics whose relationships with organizations are little more than a workshop or a corporate campaign, I developed these concepts while working at changing organizations over long periods of time: AT&T, 22 years; Volvo, 15 years; ABB, 12 years; Swedbank, 15 years; US State Department, 12 years. I have also had multi-year engagements with other companies, unions, universities, and the World Bank.

My experience has made me question the approaches to change commonly taught in business schools. Typically, they present a formula or road map like John Kotter's much-cited eight-step model.[1] I found that different approaches fit different contexts. No single formula fits the different reasons for change and different strategies indicated. Sometimes there is a burning platform that ignites change, but even without a burning platform creative leaders understand threats and opportunities in the business environment and envision changes that improve products, productivity, and the quality of service. Sometimes change is necessary to retain key customers. And sometimes, new technology requires organizational change to improve productivity. I have experienced all these kinds of change, and rather than linear steps on a road map, they required interactive, iterative processes to move an organization toward an ideal future (see Chapter 5). They also required understanding the cultural context of organizations and the melodies that harmonize with the motivational values of people at work.

To change organizations, leaders have to engage the intrinsic motivation of collaborators. Material incentives have never been enough; they are even demotivating when people focus on maximizing the money they make rather than *what* they make or *do* for customers (see Chapter 7). Neither employees nor customers are inspired when a company's sole purpose is profit. But when the purpose is improving the lives of people, now and in the future, companies are more likely to gain and retain customers, recruit and engage talented people, and increase profitability. To do this, leaders need to formulate and communicate a meaningful purpose and practice values that are essential to achieve that purpose, reinforced by what is measured. To become effective, these values have to be interpreted and practiced throughout the organization (see Chapter 4).

The typical business school formula also assumes a single model of leadership. But different types of leaders, working together, have effectively led

Table P.1. Seven approaches to organizational change

Typical business school approach	What's wrong?	Alternative approach
Single formula	Different approaches are needed in different situations	Start with purpose and context and customize
Linear steps	Ignores interactions	Interactive process toward implementing a systemic vision
Motivation by material incentives	Doesn't engage collaboration	Engage collaboration by connecting to intrinsic motives
Purpose is profit	Doesn't inspire employees or focus on customers	Purpose is gaining and retaining customers and talented collaborators by improving their effectiveness and quality of life to achieve sustainable profitability
Values dictated from the top	Values not connected to purpose and not remembered or followed	All employees participate in proposing and implementing values that further organization's purpose
Single leadership model	Different types of leaders needed	Strategic, operational, and network leaders work together
Bottom line measurement of success	Short-term thinking	Measures of achieving purpose and practicing values that sustain success

change. These are strategic, operational, and networking leaders. They have different roles, personalities, and leadership qualities (see Chapter 3).

These business school formulas typically measure change by the bottom line. This is short-term thinking. Sustainable change requires measures that support the purpose and values of the organization. Table P.1 describes seven approaches to organization change, the typical business school approach, what's wrong with it, and an alternative approach that is described in this book.

I will show in this book that without the qualities of strategic intelligence and what W. Edwards Deming termed "profound knowledge," leaders are not likely to succeed in their change efforts. And with these qualities, they will be better able draw their own road maps and master the tools essential to lead change.

Knowledge for Change

Strategic intelligence combines different kinds of knowledge not usually found in one person. These include knowledge of products, systems, processes, personality, motivation, and how knowledge is created. Leadership teams need to unite this knowledge by recruiting people with different abilities and creating a collaborative culture.

When I began to work with leaders of change, I brought knowledge from psychology and anthropology. My academic background led to an interest in the relation between personality and work, how we are motivated to work, how we think about our work, and how work shapes the values that drive our behavior. As an undergraduate at Harvard, I studied cognitive psychology and motivation with Jerome S. Bruner, who supervised my research on how the interaction of personality factors and incentives influence thinking.[2] Bruner was my mentor in learning research methodology.

My studies in cultural anthropology convinced me that both personality and cognition (perception, thinking, memory) are to a large degree shaped by culture. With Clyde Kluckhohn at Harvard, I studied the ways in which different cultures influence what people perceive, name, and remember. During a post-graduate year at New College, Oxford on a Woodrow Wilson Fellowship, my knowledge of culture was expanded in a seminar on African societies, led by E. E. Evans-Pritchard.

In 1955, David Riesman invited me to be a teaching assistant in his course on the classics of social science at the College of the University of Chicago. Riesman was a sociologist who used the concepts and methods of cultural anthropology in his studies of American culture and personality. After a year at Chicago, where I also participated in seminars with Robert Redfield in anthropology, Bruno Bettelheim in psychoanalysis, and Leo Strauss on Machiavelli, I returned to Harvard to complete my doctorate. Two years later, Riesman became a Harvard professor and we continued to work together.

In 1960, Riesman and I published an article titled "The American Crisis".[3] It was during the height of the Cold War, and attacks on communists, former communists, and so-called fellow travelers had caused many Americans to fear expressing idealistic views that might turn up in some party line. Americans were turning away from progressive visions. Riesman and I argued that Americans needed a meaningful vision beyond self-indulgent consumerism or puritanical conservatism. We suggested a focus on civil rights and on work that stimulates the worker's creative potential and industry that designs work so that it has a positive impact on worker families, communities, and political life.

I had been inspired by a meeting with Edwin Land, the founder of Polaroid, who had redesigned production work so that workers expanded their jobs and shared management functions. His goal was to engage intrinsic motivation and develop worker skills. Riesman and I saw Land's experiments as a model for transforming industrial work.

Riesman introduced me to Erich Fromm (1900–1980), the psychoanalyst and social thinker who had written about the importance of meaningful work to mental health.[4] Fromm was living in Mexico, directing the Mexican Institute of Psychoanalysis and initiating a study of Mexican villagers, aimed at understanding the relationship between personality, work, and mental health. Fromm was looking for a research associate with knowledge of statistics and psychological testing. I was looking for training in psychoanalysis for two reasons: one, I viewed psychoanalysis as the best method of understanding human motivation; and two, I wanted a profession that would support independence. I was not only attracted to Fromm as a teacher, but also because we were both engaged in the movement for nuclear disarmament.

In 1960, with a doctorate from Harvard in Social Relations (combining clinical psychology and cultural anthropology) and a research and training fellowship from the National Institute of Mental Health, with my wife, I drove from Cambridge, Massachusetts to Mexico. For eight years, I studied and worked with Fromm and eventually practiced and taught psychoanalysis in Mexico and co-authored *Social Character in a Mexican Village*.[5]

When I led a change project with a group of adolescents in the Mexican Village, the purpose was to equip the boys with new skills: raising animals and selling chickens, eggs, and pork in the market. The only conceptual skills I brought were those of cultural anthropology and psychology. They equipped me to be a participant observer, to listen to the villagers, and to ask questions to try to understand how the villagers viewed the world and what motivated them. The study of anthropology directed me to explore the history of the village, how cultural patterns were shaped, and how the village was adapting to change.

Our study showed that a large part of personality, what Fromm termed the *social character*, is shaped by peasant culture to adapt the peasant to a farming-craft mode of production that hadn't changed for centuries. Deviations from this adaptive social character helped to explain both social pathology such as alcoholism and violence, and entrepreneurial activity that was changing the village and others like it.

The understanding of personality and social character gained from my work with Fromm has informed my studies of leadership and motivation at work and the concepts presented in Chapters 6 and 7.

The Mexican study was the start of a journey that led from research to practice in changing organizations. In that journey, I had the good fortune to learn from three innovative thinkers: Einar Thorsrud, Russell Ackoff, and W. Edwards Deming. Einar Thorsrud (1923–1985) directed the Norwegian Work Research Institute and the national project on Participation at Work, sponsored by government, employers, and unions. He was a psychologist who developed his ideas on participation together with Eric Trist and Fred Emery at the Tavistock Institute in London. Russell Ackoff (1919–2009) was professor of management science at the Wharton School, University of Pennsylvania. He was a pioneer in operations research and systems thinking. He brought to his work in organizations a background in architecture and philosophy. W. Edwards Deming (1900–1993) is best known for his work with leaders of Japanese industry after World War II. He is credited with inspiring the rise of that industry based on the development of quality manufacturing. His background was in engineering, physics, and statistics. In the chapters that follow, I will refer to what I learned from these thinkers, each of whom brought knowledge from other fields to the study of organizations.

When I returned to the United States in 1968, with a fellowship at the Center for Advanced Study in the Behavioral Sciences at Stanford and support from the Harvard Program on Technology and Society, I applied the theory and methods of social character to study leadership and work in companies producing advanced technology. I was able to interview managers and engineers at companies such as IBM, HP, Intel, TI, and Dupont. A major reason I was invited in was that I promised to share my findings with them, and they wanted to understand themselves better.

The research attempted to answer these questions:

1. What are the values and social character of the leaders in the forefront of developing the new information technology that is changing the mode of production in the most advanced countries? Do these leaders care about the impact of what they produce on people and the environment?

2. What is the social character of followers and what motivates them at work?

3. How does work shape personality? What qualities are reinforced?

4. How can work be changed to further human development?

This book includes answers to these questions that I continue to discover through research, practice and teaching.

Plan of the Book

Chapter 1 describes my learning journey from studying leadership and work to playing a leadership role and developing conceptual tools for leading change.

Chapter 2 describes strategic intelligence, a conceptual system that prepares leaders to create an effective change process. Strategic intelligence includes foresight, visioning, partnering, and motivating. Exercising these qualities requires that leaders articulate an organizational philosophy and master knowledge of systems, variation, psychology, and the development of knowledge.

Chapter 3 describes the changing context of production that requires organizational change and how different kinds of leaders—strategic, operational, networking—interact in the change process.

In Chapter 4, we see that effective leaders of change articulate and communicate a philosophy that guides the organization, including organizational purpose, practical values that support that purpose, the ethical and moral basis of decision making, and measurement of results consistent with purpose and values.

Chapter 5 presents Russell Ackoff's concepts of systems thinking, idealized design, and interactive planning. These are conceptual tools I have used and elaborated in effective change projects.

Leaders of interactive planning are more effective when they understand themselves and the personalities and motivation of the people they need as collaborators. What are their strengths? What is their intrinsic motivation? Chapter 6 presents theory and methods of understanding self and others.

Chapter 7 describes how to employ *smart motivation* that combines hard incentives with the softer style of engaging the intrinsic drives of people at work. This chapter presents the conceptual tools of the 5Rs that motivate: reasons, responsibilities, recognition, rewards, and relationships.

Chapter 8 presents learning from W. Edwards Deming's concepts of transformation and profound knowledge compared and contrasted with Ackoff's concepts. This chapter also considers the relationship between national character and organizational culture.

Chapter 9 reflects on how to build on the work of Ackoff, Deming, and Fromm to understand and develop great organizations.

How can strategic intelligence be developed? The appendix provides exercises that have proved useful.

Notes

1. John Kotter, *Leading Change* (Boston: Harvard Business School Press, 1996).
2. Michael Maccoby, *Concept Formation and the Pay-off Matrix*, unpublished honors thesis, Harvard College, 1954.
3. David Riesman and Michael Maccoby, "The American Crisis," *Commentary* (June 1960), 461–72.
4. Erich Fromm, *The Sane Society* (New York: Rinehart, 1955).
5. Erich Fromm and Michael Maccoby, *Social Character in a Mexican Village* (Englewood Cliffs, NJ: Prentice-Hall, 1970, reprinted with new introduction by Michael Maccoby, New Brunswick: Transaction Publishers, 1996).

Contents

List of Figures

List of Tables

1

Introduction: Learning from Practice

Learning without labor is barren; it does nothing to better the world.
Labor without learning is empty; it does nothing to enlighten the world.
If you carry on the good work of your predecessors, their merit will sustain you.

—Wisdom of the Fathers

When I started research on leadership and work in 1969, I returned to the issues of industrial work that David Reisman and I had explored a decade before. During its course, I met some of the leading thinkers and practitioners of organization change, who included me in their meetings, and this led me to a new career as an agent of change. Eventually a business leader asked me to aid him in humanizing work, and others followed.

These idealistic leaders were the exceptions. Most of the managers I interviewed did not worry about the impact of work on the wellbeing of workers, or of their products on society. Those at the top were focused on growth and profit. They were not willing to take actions they believed would put them at a competitive disadvantage. Their view was that government should make rules that all companies have to follow to protect people and the environment. Lower-level managers mainly thought about meeting budgets and improving productivity.[1]

The best companies I studied treated their professional employees well and invested in their development. Workers were well paid, but factory work was organized according to Tayloristic principles, narrow, mind-numbing, repetitive tasks. Although company surveys indicated that most workers were satisfied with their jobs, interviews by Alejandro Cordoba, a psychoanalyst and my research associate, showed that workers might not be conscious of the damage to their health caused by Tayloristic work.

One worker who stated that he was satisfied with his work had the job of tightening screws of the suspension of a car in the same way hundreds of times a day. Despite his stated job satisfaction, he complained that he often felt stressed and anxious at the factory and tended to take it out on other workers.

When he returned home, he felt exhausted and irritated, not the case when he had worked at a small craft shop, repairing cars at his own pace, analyzing and solving problems. He also reported that since he had begun working in the factory, he suffered from constant headaches, frequent colds, and colitis. These symptoms suggested an unconscious conflict between what he consciously thought—that his work was satisfying—and what he unconsciously knew—that his work was infuriating and destructive to his body and spirit. This conflict appeared in a repetitive dream he told to Dr Cordoba.

He said, "I dream that at my work there is a man who is a stranger and we are arguing. I don't know who he is, and I don't remember what I am arguing with him about." This dream suggests why this worker did not connect his anger and symptoms to his work. Unconsciously, the worker is two people, one the conscious self who is satisfied at work, the other the unconscious "stranger" who has a different point of view. What are these two aspects of the self arguing about? The dreamer can't remember. But the evidence from the interview suggests that the stranger is telling the dreamer that he has to leave this workplace to become whole and healthy. That this knowledge is repressed is fully understandable when we learn that the worker needs this job to support his family and cannot imagine any way of changing the production process.[2] Although this was just one worker, I soon had evidence that many workers were objecting to alienating work.

In 1969, I moved my family to Washington D.C., where I met Neil Herrick at the US Labor Department and Harold Sheppard at the W. E. Upjohn Institute for Employment Research. Both shared my view that Taylorisitic factory work was bad for workers. Sheppard had data in support. He had surveyed workers and discovered that those with more education complained about mindless work.[3] However, there were promising examples of redesigned work that engaged workers and stimulated their development. Fred Foulkes, then at the Harvard Business School, introduced us to experiments in the humanization of work. Lou Davis at UCLA and Richard Walton at the Harvard Business School were consulting to leaders who were transforming continuous process work in oil refineries, paper and pulp mills, and food-processing plants. The reasoning these leaders gave for changing work was mostly economic, that by increasing worker knowledge and authority, workers would be able to stop and reprogram a process that was unsafe or producing poor-quality products. But the consultants and managers were also proud that they were improving the workers' skills and job satisfaction.

In 1971, with Herrick's help, I organized a one-day symposium on Technology and the Humanization of Work at the annual meeting of the American Association for the Advancement of Science. Sheppard, Herrick, and Foulkes had pointed out that the large unions ignored, even resisted, efforts to improve the quality of working life. In an effort to recruit a major union, I invited Doug Fraser, then vice president of the United Auto Workers (UAW) and later president, to a planning meeting at my house. Fraser was supportive, but he said that I needed to know more about workers. I was too theoretical and idealistic. He invited me to interview workers at a UAW convention, visit a GM factory, and meet union officials at their Black Lake, Michigan learning center.

What I learned fit Sheppard's findings. Some workers did not complain about working on the assembly line. Their complaints were about forced overtime and lack of breaks. But others expressed dissatisfaction with the monotonous work and had ideas to improve it.

Although many factory workers were satisfied to have a well-paying job in the early 1970s, automobile workers were complaining about speed-ups and some were sabotaging the assembly line, even putting coke bottles in gas tanks. Some were also complaining about the shoddy quality of the cars they were building.

At the AAAS symposium, corporate leaders and consultants described some of the new projects to improve work. A group of protesters from Science for the People tried to shout them down, saying that humanizing work was a new way to pacify workers and delay the revolution, but I was able to quieten them with the promise that I would let them present a critique after the presentations. There was not much of a critique; they had to admit that workers were benefitting from the changes.

Because of the interest generated by the symposium, the Labor Department organized a series of seminars to promote projects like the ones presented at the meeting. Managers, union leaders, academics, and government officials participated.

The Bolivar Project

Around that time, Sidney Harman, an idealistic CEO who was a pioneer in the high-fidelity industry, heard me lecture and asked me to help him "humanize" one of his factories that produced auto parts in Bolivar, Tennessee, where workers were represented by the UAW. Irving Bluestone, a UAW vice president who had attended one of the seminars, was skeptical, but after I described the project and vouched for Harman to UAW leaders at the union's headquarters in Detroit, they agreed to sponsor the project. I then needed to find a project director. Eric Trist, who I met at a meeting of change agents, suggested I ask Einar Thorsrud, and he arranged for me to meet Thorsrud in Oslo. In the summer of 1973, I traveled with my wife and four children to Oslo, met

Thorsrud, and invited him to direct the Bolivar project. He said he had too much to do in Norway, but that since both parties trusted me, I should direct the project and he would mentor me.

Agent of Change

So began the start of the new career as an agent of change. Thorsrud kept his promise. Not only did he mentor me, he later also mentored some of the fellows in a program I directed at the Kennedy School at Harvard that had been funded by Harman, grateful for the results at Bolivar. The project had not only increased his company's profits, but also given him national recognition, and was the reason President Jimmy Carter appointed him Deputy Secretary of Commerce in 1977.

Workers at the Bolivar factory were invited to propose new ways of doing their jobs with the promise that if they met quotas, they could leave work early or take courses in work-related skills such as welding and in subjects some of them requested, including public speaking and piano playing. As a result, the work became more interesting, and they were motivated to improve productivity. The new collaboration between management and union also resulted in an agreement to cut costs to win a contract and then share the profits.

Because of the Bolivar Project's success, I was invited to join new projects. Berth Jönsson, HR vice president of Volvo, engaged me to work with a team of managers, engineers, and union officials designing a factory in Uddevalla, Sweden, where teams of workers would assemble cars without an assembly line. Harman bought the Tannoy loudspeaker company in the UK and was moving production from London to Coatbridge near Glasgow. In 1975, at a conference on the future of work at Ditchley Park near Oxford, my description of the Bolivar Project interested a leader of the General and Municipal Workers Union (now GMB), who liked the idea of union–management collaboration to improve work, and the Labour Government's Department of Employment also supported the project.

When Harman became Deputy Secretary at Commerce, he appointed Elsa Porter as Assistant Secretary of Administration, and she engaged me to initiate a work redesign project in the printing department to show that the principles of employee participation pioneered in industry were equally effective in government.[4] I also found they were effective when I facilitated a change project with garbage collectors in Springfield, Ohio that improved productivity and labor relations. Employees in trucks offered to call others when they finished a run and help those who were still working. Management agreed that all reductions in force would be by attrition, not lay-offs.

In 1978, I was invited to address the top executives of AT&T and the Bell System, then a regulated monopoly with one million employees, on possibilities for improving work relationships. Surveys were showing that workers were disengaged, which had a negative impact on productivity. Bob Gaynor, an AT&T Long Lines vice president, invited me to work with him in Kansas City. In *Agents of Change*, I describe how his support for union–management collaboration was the first step in gaining union cooperation to improve the quality of work life and quality of service for a program I led for the whole Bell system.[5]

The work improvement projects of the 1970s and 1980s improved productivity, product quality, and labor relations, and increased employee engagement. But none of them lasted. They were too encapsulated in a department or factory and too dependent on consultants. The Norwegians had hoped that once companies saw the results of their demonstration projects in factories they would want to copy them. But we learned that changes in a factory or department would be sustained only if they fit a total organizational system redesign. Furthermore, these projects did not make use of the advanced thinking about changing work developed by Deming, Joseph Juran, and Taiichi Ohno of Toyota that were beginning to spread in Japan.

Perhaps the main reason quality-of-working-life programs have disappeared is that companies no longer need to improve factory work to recruit semi-skilled workers. Some of the work has been automated. Some has been outsourced to low-wage countries, where workers are happy to have any job with a decent wage. Management seems unconcerned that Gallup surveys show most employees are not engaged at work. Today, the assembly line is back in Volvo factories, together with some Japanese processes to improve productivity, with the result that worker stress has increased.[6]

In 2006, at an international meeting on intervention practices to change firms, sponsored by ANACT, the French National Agency for the Improvement of Working Conditions, researchers and change agents from Europe and North America discussed efforts to improve both productivity and the quality of working life. Despite successful programs in Finland and Quebec, they concluded that in the context of globalization and intense competition, there has been increased centralization and pressure on workers.[7] With the diminished clout of unions, there are few champions promoting the quality of working life unless it can be proved that it is essential for effectiveness or for recruiting talented knowledge workers.

Unions and Change

When we began the movement to improve the quality of working life in the US, the unions were barriers to change. In 1973, when Berth Jönsson and I met at a conference organized by the students at Principia College in Southern Illinois, we had similar views on the virtues of work improvement, but the president of the machinists union expressed the views of most union leaders that a fattened pay check was the only improvement workers wanted. Doug Fraser and Irving Bluestone of the UAW were the first union officials to support work improvement projects in the US. Bluestone saw the projects as not only improving the wellbeing of workers, but also as a step toward industrial democracy, increasing the power of workers and their unions. During the 1970s, Bluestone was able to apply the Bolivar model of work improvement to a number of GM and Ford factories.

In 1980, Glenn Watts, president of the Communication Workers of America (CWA), asked me to design a quality-of-working-life program for his members at AT&T and the Bell System, and the company agreed to launch the program and hire me to direct it, paid 50–50 by company and union.[8] Watts also asked me to facilitate a meeting of the union executive board on improving collaboration among union leaders. As a result, some of the union vice presidents asked me to facilitate this kind of meeting with their staff.

Working with union leadership, I learned that it took courage for union officials to collaborate with management. Unions are democratic organizations. Leaders who collaborate are vulnerable to losing elections to opponents who accuse them of being in bed with management. It is easier to explain what may be gained by opposition than to explain what may be achieved by collaboration.

Furthermore, possibilities for union–management collaboration run up against a catch-22 situation. Managements are only interested in collaborating with a union because otherwise it could hurt them with its militancy. However, managements don't want to collaborate with a militant union that has hurt them with grievances, slow-downs, and strikes.

Yet I have worked with visionary managers and courageous union leaders who saw that collaboration could improve the working life of members and even gain new members for a union, as CWA did in right-to-work states where workers do not have to join a union, even though it has been voted in by a majority of the workers. Watts' successor, Morton Bahr was at first resistant to collaboration, but after he joined me in visits to AT&T workplaces and saw that workers were enthusiastic about the program, he became an active supporter.

In countries with strong unions like Scotland in the 1970s and Sweden throughout the time I worked there from 1975 to 2000, union leaders were confident partners with management. As a consultant to Swedbank, I brought the union president, Kaissa Bratt, into the bank's strategic discussions, and she provided frontline knowledge that improved Göran Collert's business strategy and its implementation.

In the US during the 1980s and 90s, I worked with two other unions, the Bricklayers and Allied Craftsmen (BAC) and the American Federation of Teachers (AFT). Both had visionary leaders: Jack Joyce of BAC and Al Shanker of AFT. Both of these leaders had goals of strengthening their unions and increasing the competence of their members, and also the quality of their products.

Joyce engaged Quinn Mills of the Harvard Business School and me to facilitate a process to strengthen the union and the masonry industry. Joyce reasoned that there were hundreds of small masonry contractors, and the union could be the integrating organization. Together with leaders of the masonry contractors' organization, he established the Masonry Institute to fund marketing, research and development, and training so that masonry would be better equipped to compete against other building materials.

Shanker supported collaboration with school officials to improve education. He had the foresight to see that teaching had to change to prepare students for the age of knowledge work. He had the idea of charter schools as laboratories of innovation for public schools. AFT was dominated by the division of K-12 teachers, but also had divisions of higher-education teachers, government employees, nurses and other healthcare workers, and other school employees. I was engaged to facilitate the process with union leadership of designing a strategy and structure for the union. AFT had to integrate the different membership groups so that each retained some autonomy, with the combined leadership able to represent the whole union on policy issues. Using a variation of Ackoff's model of idealized design and with the help of AFT staff, I designed a new structure and discussed it in meetings with over 1,000 AFT local leaders. The strategic plan was approved by the union's convention. The current AFT president, Randi Weingarten, has continued to support Shanker's vision of collaboration.

Since the time I worked with them, unions in the US and Europe have continued to lose members, especially in the private sector. They remain strong in some areas, such as government- and state-owned companies. In 2013, I met with managers and union leaders who were fighting each other at Petrotrin, the oil company that contributes 40 percent of Trinidad and Tobago's revenue. I found the same main issue that undermined collaboration in other organizations I worked with—lack of respect from management for workers and the union, resulting in lack of respect by the union for management. Workers and local union leaders can contribute knowledge and support to improve production. When unions cooperate, they are a better alternative to defend the interests of workers than government regulators or outside lawyers who have no interest in the company's success. But their role as representatives of workers for salary, benefits, and health and safety has to be respected by management. Furthermore, if managers educate union leaders about the business and its strategy, they become better able to help. When respected, the unions I've worked with have been flexible about issues such as seniority and work rules that impede productivity.

Of course, there are corrupt, incompetent, and inflexible union leaders just as there are exploitative, incompetent, and inflexible managers. However, while unions appear to be slipping on a slope to oblivion, there have been times before when they seemed to be finished, only to rise again.

Transforming Knowledge Work

In the 1980s, companies were forced to change to meet the challenge of global competition. To compete, large US companies like GM and AT&T, which had dominated their markets, had to cut costs and improve quality. In 1984, a court decree broke the Bell System into AT&T and seven regional telephone operating systems. I remained with AT&T for another 16 years, and together with Charles Heckscher and Sue Schurman, led a program in the 1990s called Workplace of the Future, described in our book *Agents of Change*. Using Russell Ackoff's model of designing an ideal system, we were able to engage managers and workers to collaborate in changing work in ways that significantly improved productivity and customer service, while also improving motivation and opportunities for learning.

At the end of the 1980s, I began to use new instruments for organizational transformation. Ackoff not only taught me to use systems thinking to design an idealized future for an organization, but also invited me to join him in workshops on change with managers of the Canadian Pacific Corporation. (For discussions of systems thinking and idealized design, see Chapters 2 and 5 in this volume.) W. Edwards Deming, the statistician who helped inspire the Japanese to transform their industries into models for the world, introduced me to the concepts and knowledge required for organizational transformation.

Because of the lessons I learned from Deming and Ackoff, the change projects I worked on in the 1990s and the twenty-first century were designed systemically and built on firmer foundations than the earlier projects. I was invited to work with other companies that, like AT&T, were being pressured by competition and customer demands to transform bureaucratic organizations into collaborative learning organizations.

In 1988, a merger of the Swedish and Swiss electrical products companies, Asea and Brown Boveri created the global giant ABB. At the start, managers from different countries accused each other of failure to cooperate. Goran Lindahl, an EVP who later became CEO, asked me to study the causes of distrust and conflict.[9] My success in improving collaboration between managers in different countries resulted in them inviting me to facilitate meetings to resolve conflicts among them.

In 1994, Lindahl asked me to try to figure out why the Canadian company was in the red and what could be done about it. I suggested that members of the executive team interview their major customers in metal and mining, electric utilities, and paper production (pulp and paper) to ask how ABB might better meet their needs.

ABB's products were becoming "commodities," undifferentiated products with disappearing profit margins, but their larger customers were willing to spend a lot more on solutions and results than on products. COMINCO in Western Canada, the largest zinc producer in the world, wanted ABB to produce cheaper and cleaner energy for them. But this demanded changes in ABB's organization, mode of production, and reward system. ABB was organized into many business units incentivized to maximize profitability on products. To meet COMINCO's request, engineers and technicians from different units would have to collaborate with each other and with the customer's experts. In *The Leaders We Need*, I describe using Ackoff's tools for system redesign and facilitating an interactive process for managers to change processes and incentives to develop a collaborative culture.[10]

Around this time, I had a similar assignment at the MITRE Corporation. MITRE (from MIT Research) was founded as a fully funded federal research and development center (FFRDC). FFRDCs were authorized by Congress to be able to pay higher salaries than would be possible in the government. This was necessary to attract the best engineers and technical personnel in the country to provide advanced products and services to the Strategic Air Command, the air traffic control system of the Federal Aviation Administration (FAA), and other government agencies. In my book *Why Work*, I reported interviews with air traffic controllers who complained about the management system and the stress of their jobs.[11] Jack Fearnsides, the MITRE vice president for the FAA, read the book and asked me to help him lead change.

MITRE's customers complained that MITRE was throwing technology at them rather than working with them to solve their problems. When I went with Fearnsides to ask the FAA administrator what he wanted from MITRE, he said, "We have more radar than we can use. What we need is help in getting the pilots and controllers to cooperate."

Fearnsides introduced me to Barry Horowitz, the CEO who supported a 5-year project to study client needs and transform the organizational system from a rigid bureaucracy to a collaborative, customer-responsive community.

In these change projects, I was no longer focusing on the liberation of workers from the chains of Taylorism. Without having planned it, I had become a consultant for changing knowledge organizations from the production of products to "products wrapped in solutions," to borrow a phrase used by Sam Palmisano, the CEO of IBM, who led this kind of transformation at IBM at the beginning of the twenty-first century.

I was learning about the factors that were forcing knowledge-service organizations to change, to transform traditional bureaucracies into learning organizations. My experiences with ABB and MITRE taught me that customers were the key to motivating a company to change from a bureaucratic producer into a collaborative provider of solutions. My learning was facilitated by discussions with Ackoff, Deming, Pierre-Eric Tixier, Rafael Ramirez, and Charles Heckscher, who also organized a group of consultants and researchers who met periodically to share views about change.[12]

The following are key principles I learned about changing a knowledge-service organization from a bureaucracy to a collaborative learning organization.

- Productivity depends on co-production, collaboration. It cannot be controlled by the organization alone. ABB and MITRE had to learn to work collaboratively with their customers. This principle obviously applies to professional service. An accountant's productivity depends on a client keeping good records. A physician's productivity depends on the patient taking the medicine prescribed, sticking to a diet, or exercising.

- An effective knowledge-service organization is a *social system* where all the parts must interact to achieve the system's purpose.

- People who are parts of a social system have purposes of their own. Leadership is essential to create a common purpose and engage co-workers in a collaborative, interactive enterprise.

Leadership for Change—Research, Coaching, Teaching

Effective change, no matter where it starts in an organization, requires leadership. Since 1970, I have studied leaders, and starting in 2003, I have led classes and workshops with the goal of developing leadership to be effective in terms of both economic and human values.

My book *The Leader* (1981)[13] described some of the business, union, and government leaders I worked with in the 1970s at different levels of their organizations who were changing these organizations and improving work in the US, UK, and Sweden. P. G. Gyllenhammar, Volvo CEO, was one of the leaders I profiled. He was also chairman of the board of FArådet (The Swedish Council for Management and Worklife Issues), a think tank funded by the Employers Confederation. The board approved his suggestion that I be invited to study Swedish leadership and describe the kind of leaders Sweden would need in the future.

I was happy to accept this unique opportunity to interview Sweden's leaders. At a meeting with the board, one member, a business school professor, said that one reason they were engaging me was that no Swedish academic would take on a study like this, because leadership was not an academic discipline. The results would not be published in any prestigious academic journal and would not improve a researcher's chances for promotion.

In the early 1980s, when I lectured on *The Leader* at the Kennedy School, leftist students criticized my "elitist" focus on leadership. They argued that change should be led collaboratively. Their ideal was worker cooperatives. In contrast, students at the Harvard Business School invited me to discuss the book with them. They complained that even though leadership was obviously essential for business success, no one at the school was teaching it. Of course, this has changed dramatically, and leadership courses now abound at every business school and school of public administration. I think the reason for this is that increased global competition forced companies to change, and effective change requires leaders.

Sweden became my laboratory for learning about different types of leaders and observing how they functioned over time.

With researchers at FArådet, I interviewed Swedish leaders of business, government, and unions. We found the most common leadership model was the *expert*, who analyzed problems and made decisions about solutions based on what had worked well in the past. These leaders lacked vision and were resistant to change. They were unprepared for the growing global competitive market that had already destroyed Sweden's shipping industry and threatened other mainstay industries.

After World War II, when their European competitors had been devastated, Swedish industry was unchallenged and had become prosperous and complacent. Expert leadership worked well when there was little need for innovation. With competition, Sweden needed new kinds of leaders, and we found a few successful innovators in business and government.

We published our findings in Swedish in *Ledare for Sverge* (*Leaders for Sweden*), and my reports about our findings were published in *Dagens Nyheter*,

Sweden's largest newspaper and in *Sweden at the Edge*, a collection of essays I edited on leadership in Sweden.[14]

Ten years later, Gyllenhammar and Jan Carlzon of SAS, the most innovative Swedish business leaders we described, had lost their jobs and with them, the adulation of the Swedish public. On 26 January 1995, my analysis of what happened to these leaders was translated into Swedish and published in *Dagans Nyheter*, entitled "Den Karismatika Fällan" ("The Fallen Charismatics"). By observing what had happened to these leaders, I gained an understanding of the dynamics of charismatic leadership and the importance of Freud's concept of the narcissistic personality in explaining visionary leadership. What I wrote then applies to many visionary leaders who become the object of public adulation:

> What produces a charismatic leader? The official cultural norm is that Swedish leaders should not give themselves airs. Leaders should be first among equals, distinguished by their demonstrated expertise. The law of Jante is meant to punish the leader who tries to stand too far above the group. Yet in the 80s, Sweden began to glorify industrial leaders, particularly Gyllenhammar and Carlzon who were treated with the kind of public adulation, TV interviews and magazine cover stories, reserved for world celebrities like ABBA, Bjorn Borg, and Ingemar Stenmark. Now, suddenly these stars have fallen. What happened?
>
> From the business economists' point of view, the answer lies in dramatic success followed by bad results in the case of Carlzon and an unfavorable deal with Renault in the case of Gyllenhammar. But Gyllenhammar had made bad deals before this, and the problems of SAS preceded the fall of Carlzon by several years. What was different this time? From a psychoanalytic point of view, a complex drama seems to have played out between these leaders and the Swedish people, leading to their downfall.
>
> Charisma is not merely an individual quality. It flowers from a relationship between leader and followers. Both Gyllenhammar and Carlzon were innovators. As Freud pointed out, those leaders who are able to break old molds and forge new models must have strong elements of the narcissistic character. Like the other character types he described, the narcissist has both positive and negative potentialities. Which of these predominate may depend on the playing out of relationships with others. Based in part on a Rorschach test, I wrote in *The Leader* (1981) that Gyllenhammar's weakness was his narcissism and in *Why Work* (1988) referred to this element in Carlzon's character as typical for innovators. Although the narcissist sometimes undervalues reality and may hide out in his own world of ideas, if affirmed by the public, he expands and glows. Applause and adulation bolster his self-confidence and conviction that his innovative views are correct, as well they may be. As he gains trust in his intuitions, his self-assurance and spontaneity, his direct responsiveness, delight his audience and create the illusion that he is in touch with them. He has become charismatic and can do no wrong. He can realize his deepest fantasies of being free of all constraints.

The most dramatic innovations by Gyllenhammar and Carlzon had a populist appeal and also resulted in worldwide acclaim for Sweden. Gyllenhammar appeared to revolutionize industrial work, to replace the dehumanizing assembly line of Chaplin's *Modern Times* with a Swedish and worldwide labor ideal of team-based craftwork. Carlzon was the pioneer of what has become a global re-engineering of service work, combining customer focus and frontline empowerment. The praise and publicity showered on these leaders by the international business press and analysts, including this writer, spilled over to feed the group narcissism of the Swedish people, the feeling of being special and superior to other people. Even though they were sometimes criticized as too self-promoting, Gyllenhammar and Carlzon were given special dispensation to break the law of Jante, because they glorified Sweden to the world and seemed also to strengthen egalitarian, humanistic values.

But the same adulation that satisfies narcissistic needs also has a destructive effect on the leader. As he expands, breaking barriers and crossing boundaries, he no longer listens to cautious words of advice. After all, he has been right before, when others were disbelieving. Rather than trying to persuade those who disagree with him, he avoids conflict by ignoring them. He becomes isolated from those he must depend on for information and implementation. Thus, when some of his managers, for good or bad reasons, did not sign onto his vision in the late 1980s, Gyllenhammar said he did not expect them to share his values, as though these were personal expressions rather than, as he had said in the 1970s, good business practice.

Instead of working with his managers, listening to their concerns and gaining their buy-in, Gyllenhammar communicated with the public through the media as he turned toward new, expansive business deals. It is consistent with this that what finally undid the Renault deal was disapproval by managers whom he had neither consulted nor persuaded.

In 1989, when Carlzon's management team was asked whether they agreed with his organizational vision, one vice president, a former pilot, said, "No, I still believe the best organization is the military." Carlzon replied, "That may be true, if your goal is to shoot your customers." Carlzon's witty rejoinder did not seriously engage his subordinates in a dialogue about good organization. Furthermore, he did not put his attention to developing his innovative vision, which was in fact better done by British Airways. Carlzon did not face the issues of cost, even when many observers pointed out that SAS could not compete without improving productivity. Like Gyllenhammar's lieutenants who were skeptical about Kalmar and Uddevalla (innovative factories), Carlzon's managers could dismiss his original and creative ideas as good public relations, but impractical for managing the enterprise which they believed needed military discipline.

Like Gyllenhammar, Carlzon put his energy into an expansive strategy: hotels and alliances. Investments did not pay off, and at the same time, problems of high costs were not addressed. The frontline employees who had felt liberated and valued by Carlzon in the early 1980s felt abandoned by him ten years later.

Personality and Leadership

My observations of what had happened to Gyllenhammar and Carlzon stimulated me to explore further the relationship between personality and leadership. By reviewing my experiences with visionary leaders and seeking accounts in the business press and history books, I found a pattern. Visionary narcissistic leaders emerge in times of social upheaval and the development of disruptive technology. They can work for the common good, like Lincoln, Franklin Delano Roosevelt, and Nelson Mandela, or in a way that is ultimately destructive, like Napoleon, Hitler, and Stalin. In business, some succeed, like Henry Ford, John D. Rockefeller, and Steve Jobs, and some overreach and fail; their names are not remembered. Even the most effective narcissistic leaders can be insulting and dismissive. They use people and discard them when they are no longer useful. In *Narcissistic Leaders*, the lead article in the January 2000 issue of the *Harvard Business Review* I presented these observations. It connected with the business community and won a McKinsey award as one of the best articles of the year. In 2003, *The Productive Narcissist* was published and in 2007 re-published with a new introduction by the Harvard Business School Press as *Narcissistic Leaders, Who Succeeds and Who Fails*, along with *The Leaders We Need, and What Makes Us Follow.*[15]

In 2003, I began to teach leadership, first in the Oxford Saïd Business School-HEC executive program on Coaching and Consulting for Change. Then in 2005, I led workshops with Richard Margolies, who had applied my ideas in a week-long leadership training course for the US Army Corps of Engineers. In 2010, Tim Scudder and I developed a leadership workshop based on my writings. I have led this workshop with US executives and leaders in the UK, Egypt, Jordan, Lebanon, Kenya, and in the MPA program at Sciences Po in Paris.

I have coached leaders in companies, unions, government, and universities. One charismatic Swedish leader, Goran Collert, CEO of Swedbank, Collert encouraged me to discover the qualities of strategic intelligence that provide leaders, including productive narcissists, with tools for success in leading change.

Changing Healthcare Organizations

In the 1990s, I served the National Coalition on Health Care (NCHC), with about one hundred representatives from business, unions, pension funds, healthcare organizations, medical professional organizations, insurance companies, patient interest groups, and religious groups, as facilitator of a process to gain agreement on a national policy based on five principles: universal access to care, improved quality of care, controlled costs, equitable financing, and administrative simplification.[16] But I was and still am convinced that government policy alone cannot improve the quality and cost of health care. Since health care is knowledge-service work, I was interested in finding out if what I was learning at ABB, MITRE, and AT&T applied to improving healthcare organizations.

Paul Griner, a distinguished physician and former director of the Strong Memorial Hospital of Rochester University had been a classmate at Harvard. When I described the shift in the mode of production and organization I was experiencing at AT&T, ABB, and MITRE, he said that a similar kind of transformation of bureaucracies into collaborative communities was necessary to improve patient care and productivity in healthcare organizations. Roger Bulger, another classmate, then president of the Association of Academic Health Centers, agreed with Griner, and both encouraged me to study some of the best health organizations in the US to find out if they agreed with this diagnosis and were moving in this direction. They helped me to get a grant from the Robert Wood Johnson Foundation for a study of leadership in healthcare organizations that became the basis for consulting to healthcare organizations.

In 2013, with the collaboration of my associate Richard Margolies and Cliff and Jane Norman, who were using Deming's theories, methods, and tools to transform healthcare organizations in the US, Canada, UK, Sweden, and Singapore, we published *Transforming Health Care Leadership, A Systems Guide to Improve Patient Care, Decrease Costs, and Improve Population Health*.[17] In this book, we described how to develop these tools and others of strategic intelligence to transform healthcare bureaucracies into learning organizations.

We defined healthcare learning organizations in terms of these attributes:

- The organization is developed as a social system where all the parts interact to achieve the purpose of serving patients.
- Learning from practice is widely shared and used for innovation and improvement.
- Partnering with suppliers, client organizations, and community organizations takes place.
- Providers collaborate across disciplines with patients and their families.
- Learning is used to inform the community about the prevention of illness to improve population health.[18]

The Change of Change

Summarizing her survey of change theories, Christiane Demers concludes that over the past few decades there has been an "evolution of the field."[19] In the

1960s and 1970s, organizational change was described as management driven. In the 1980s, it was described as collective and emergent, and in the 1990s, in terms of learning organizations. What I experienced was that changes in practice responded to changes in the mode of work essential for effectiveness. Changes in theories followed changes in practice.

In the 1960s and 1970s, most bureaucracies did not change. They were presided over by cautious administrators. Only a very few innovative leaders like Harman and Gyllenhammar were changing manufacturing to improve productivity and the quality of working life. In the 1980s, with the coming of information technology, middle managers and technicians in service industries sometimes initiated change to employ new technology and serve customers. During this period, I visited AT&T technicians working with MasterCard in St Louis, Missouri. When I asked a MasterCard manager to describe the role of AT&T he said, "AT&T *is* MasterCard." AT&T provided the information systems that allowed MasterCard to transact business 24/7 and never lose a transaction. However, to maintain service, AT&T technicians had to collaborate across corporate boundaries. To do their work, they had to make quick decisions, ignoring the bureaucratic chain of command.

Starting in the 1990s, companies I worked with, such as ABB and MITRE, had to become learning organizations to provide solutions as well as products. Today, theory is again changing to describe changing practice. As Charles O'Reilly and Michael Tushman write, many companies have changed to become "ambidextrous organizations" that combine learning organizations that may innovate or collaborate with business and organizational customers with traditional production units. These units differ in processes, structures, and cultures.[20]

The types of change I have witnessed are consistent with and help to explain Demers' observation that theories have been changing. As she notes, leaders have initiated changes at different levels of their organizations. However, I have found that the most effective leaders of change have demonstrated qualities of strategic intelligence. They have had foresight and vision, have been able to partner with collaborators who complemented their abilities and knowledge, and they have been able to engage and motivate others to implement their vision. The next chapter describes these elements of strategic intelligence.

Notes

1. Michael Maccoby, *The Gamesman: The New Corporate Leaders* (New York: Simon & Schuster, 1976).
2. A. C. Cordoba, *The Human World of Work in Mexico* (Mexico City: Office of Labor Medicine and Safety, Mexican Ministry of Labor, 1976).

3. Harold L. Sheppard and Neal Q. Harrick, *Where Have All the Robots Gone?* (New York: The Free Press, 1971). Sheppard and Herrick cited Fromm's theory of social character. The study showed that more authoritarian workers were more satisfied with hierarchy and Tayloristic jobs. The authors argued that to develop a more democratic society, children should be raised and educated for work that called for reasoning, judgment, and cooperation.

4. Michael Maccoby, *The Leader: A New Face for American Management* (New York: Simon & Schuster, 1981).

5. Charles Heckscher, Michael Maccoby, Rafael Ramirez, and Pierre-Eric Tixier, *Agents of Change Crossing the Post-industrial Divide* (Oxford: Oxford University Press, 2003).

6. Jørgen Winkel, "Ergonomics and Effective Production Systems—Moving from Reactive to Proactive Development," in Julian Pelletier (ed.), *Intervention Practices in Firms* (ANACT, 2007), pp. 131–43.

7. Michael Maccoby, "Preface," in Julian Pelletier (ed.), *Intervention Practices in Firms* (ANACT, 2007), pp. 7–8.

8. This is fully described in Charles Heckscher, Michael Maccoby, Rafael Ramirez, and Pierre-Eric Tixier, *Agents of Change Crossing the Post-industrial Divide* (Oxford: Oxford University Press, 2003), ch. 3.

9. I described what I found in Michael Maccoby, *The Leaders We Need and What Makes Us Follow* (Boston, MA: Harvard Business School Press, 2007), pp. 80–2.

10. Michael Maccoby, *The Leaders We Need and What Makes Us Follow* (Boston, MA: Harvard Business School Press, 2007), pp. 100–2.

11. Michael Maccoby, *Why Work: Leading the New Generation* (New York: Simon & Schuster, 1988).

12. This group met over three years. The results were published in Charles Heckscher and Paul S. Adler, *The Firm as a Collaborative Community* (Oxford: Oxford University Press, 2006).

13. Michael Maccoby, *The Leader* (New York: Simon & Schuster, 1981).

14. Anders Edstrom, Michael Maccoby, Lennart Stromberg, and Jan Erik Rendahl, *Ledare for Sverige (Leadership for Sweden)* (Lund, Sweden: Liber, 1985).
Michael Maccoby (ed.), *Sweden at the Edge: Lessons for American and Swedish Managers* (Philadelphia, IL: University of Pennsylvania Press, 1991).

15. Michael Maccoby, "Narcissistic Leaders: The Incredible Pros, the Inevitable Cons," *Harvard Business Review*, vol. 78(1) (January–February 2000): 68–77; Michael Maccoby, *The Productive Narcissist, the Promise and Peril of Visionary Leadership* (New York: Broadway Books, 2003); Michael Maccoby, *Narcissistic Leaders, Who Succeeds and Who Fails* (Boston, MA: Harvard Business School Press, 2007); Michael Maccoby, *The Leaders We Need: And What Makes Us Follow* (Boston: Harvard Business School Press, 2007).

16. The coalition's specifications were a significant contribution to the Affordable Care Act, passed by the US Congress in 2010. However, the coalition continues to work at improving the policy's impact on costs and quality.

17. San Francisco: Jossey-Bass, 2013.

18. The concept of a learning organization was popularized by Peter M. Senge in *The Fifth Discipline* (New York: Doubleday, 1990). In *Transforming Health Care*

Leadership, our examples of learning organization are consistent with some of the qualities noted by Senge, especially systems thinking, shared vision and team learning. However, our elaboration of these concepts draws on Ackoff's definitions of systems thinking and visioning.

19. Christiane Demers, *Organizational Change Theories, A Synthesis* (Thousand Oaks, CA: Sage Publications, 2007), pp. 222–3.
20. Charles A. O'Reilly, III and Michael L. Tushman, "The Ambidextrous Organization," *Harvard Business Review*, vol. 82(4) (April 2004): 74–81.

2

Strategic Intelligence

Strategy: The art or skill of careful planning toward an advantage or desired end.
　　　　　　　　　　　　　　　　　　　　　—*Oxford English Dictionary*

Intelligence: The faculty of understanding; intellect.
　　　　　　　　　　　　　　　　　　　　　—*Oxford English Dictionary*

Both strategy and intelligence have been defined in many different ways. The elements of strategic intelligence expand on the definition in the *Oxford English Dictionary* (OED): strategy is the art or skill of careful planning toward an advantage or desired end.

In the 1980s, when oligopolistic companies like AT&T and GM controlled their markets, strategy was essentially planning, based on extrapolating from the present to the future. Strategists would estimate the future population and plan on producing enough telephones or cars to satisfy the expected demand. It did not take much intelligence to put numbers in the algorithm. But in uncertain competitive global markets with rapidly changing technology, strategists can't rely on extrapolation. They have to interpret patterns and trends and produce competitive products and services that meet customer needs. In the words of Michael Porter, they need to achieve a sustainable competitive advantage.[1] Furthermore, they need strategies to innovate and to continually improve the quality and cost of their products and services. This may require changes in processes and organization. Strategy may include partnering with key customers and suppliers. It may include having a positive social and environmental impact. To shape and implement strategies, leaders need to engage and motivate collaborators. Furthermore, to adapt to a constantly changing world, strategists must be able to learn from results, perceive threats and opportunities, preparing, if necessary, to modify their strategies. The main aim of strategy may be to design the ability to create new offerings or to adapt to new competitors, products, or technology.

This calls for the following abilities and conceptual tools (see Figure 2.1):

- *Foresight*—the ability to anticipate currents of change that can threaten an organization or provide opportunities;
- *Visioning*—the ability to design the organizational system to produce the products and services valued by customers and to continually improve processes, products, and services;
- *Partnering*—the ability to develop productive relationships, including a team with colleagues who have complementary abilities. Partnering with key customers and suppliers may also strengthen strategy;
- *Engaging, motivating,* and *empowering*—to gain collaborators who will implement the vision and continuously improve products and productivity.

To effectively practice foresight, visioning, partnering, and motivating, leaders need to develop and communicate a *philosophy* that guarantees values and guides decisions about products, partnering, organizational design and relationships with customers, collaborators, and communities. Besides knowledge of the business and its products, strategic leaders also need to master what Deming termed *profound knowledge*, including knowledge of systems, variation (statistics), motivation, and the theory of knowledge (creating and

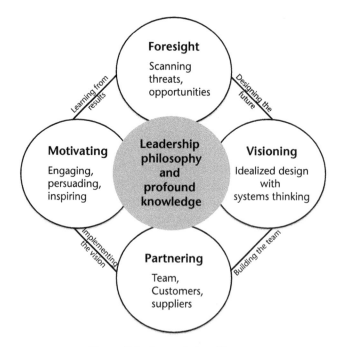

Figure 2.1. Strategic intelligence

testing ideas). This kind of knowledge is essential to empower collaborators to implement a vision, innovate, and continually improve the organization.

These skills require intellectual capabilities, thus the term strategic intelligence. The *OED* defines intelligence as understanding and intellect. However, there are different types of understanding, different sets of intellectual skills. Based on his research, Robert Sternberg, a psychologist, factored three types of intelligence: analytical, practical, and creative.[2]

- Analytic intelligence is the type tested in IQ exams. It includes analysis, memory, logic, and problem solving. Analytic intelligence is necessary, but not sufficient for strategic intelligence. Someone with only this kind of understanding and ability will do well on tests but not in relationships. That requires:

- Practical intelligence, including tact, timing, understanding people and their motives, and communicating effectively. This kind of understanding is essential for partnering and motivating, but it is not enough for foresight and visioning. That requires:

- Creative intelligence, including pattern recognition essential to making sense of changes in the business environment that either threaten or indicate opportunities for the organization. Visioning requires *systems thinking*, the ability to see the interaction of elements that combine to achieve a purpose, and imagination. Aesthetic sensibility equips a leader in many ways, including an insistence on the quality of products and presentation, customer experience, and harmony in relationships.

Russell Ackoff proposed a hierarchy of intelligence, from acquiring information to wisdom in decision making (see Figure 2.2). The hierarchy is defined as follows:

- *Data*—these are symbols that represent objects, events, and/or their properties that are products of *observation* made by people directly or with instruments like thermometers, speedometers, odometers, and voltmeters.

Figure 2.2. Hierarchy of intelligence

- *Information*—this is data processed into useful forms. Information is contained in descriptions that answer questions that begin with words like *who, what, where, when,* and *how many;*

- *Understanding*—this is the *meaning* of information. People are overwhelmed with information and often puzzled about what it means. What is the meaning of a fluctuation in sales figures or revenue? Why did hospital re-admissions increase? Understanding has to do with answers to questions like *why?* and so *what?*

- *Knowledge*—information and understanding are useful in deciding what to do but not how to do it. Knowledge implies *know-how.*

- *Wisdom*—a wise leader has the foresight to consider and evaluate the long-run consequences of decisions. For example, what will be the future consequences of cutting staff now? Is the market likely to improve? Will we need more staff in the future? Wisdom depends on understanding and knowledge, and also on a person's values.

Clearly, IQ tests don't capture the qualities described in Ackoff's hierarchy. However, the hierarchy, like traditional definitions of intelligence, lacks the qualities of emotional understanding essential for reasoned decisions. It is all head; it lacks heart. In the Old Testament, King Solomon's wisdom is based on "a heart that listens."[3] In the fourteenth century, the Moroccan philosopher, Ibn Khaldûn wrote that the concept of "heart" is central to the ability to think in a fully related way.[4] This view fits the findings of the neuroscientist Antonio Demasio, who has reported cases of people whose neo-cortex has been cut off from the emotional centers. He writes "when emotion is entirely left out of the reasoning picture . . . reason turns out to be even more flawed than when emotion plays bad tricks on our decisions."[5]

Ibn Khaldûn writes that the head is good for science, crafts, and technique, but without a developed heart, we remain in a state of vacillation. The head alone cannot resolve doubt or affirm life.

Combining head and heart, we can expand Ackoff's hierarchy as follows:

- *Data* includes emotions.

- *Information* is gained by experiencing the emotions in the context of the situation.

- *Understanding* comes from a heart that listens and understands the meaning of the emotions. It includes a sense of humor, the emotional side of a sense of reality. Life can be absurd. Someone with a sense of humor can experience the absurdity. Without a sense of humor, someone lacks understanding of reality.

- *Knowledge* includes emotional competence. For a leader, it is the ability to respond to disturbing emotions and transform them. For example, a leader may sense doubt, and fear and responding to it transform these emotions into hope and determination.

- *Wisdom* describes *judgment* that combines foresight with understanding of how decisions will affect people and courage to act according to one's values. The concept of courage comes from the Latin word for heart (*cor*). In contrast to guts, which implies taking brave, sometimes reckless risks, courage implies doing what we know is right, even when we are afraid.

Samuel Johnson made the oft quoted observation that "courage is reckoned the greatest of all virtues; because unless a man has that virtue, he has no security for preserving any other."

Elements of Strategic Intelligence

Strategic intelligence employs all these qualities of head and heart. This is how it works.

Foresight

To gain foresight, you must be able to perceive patterns that indicate threats and opportunities for your organization. Foresight is based on your subject matter knowledge, scanning the business environment, and interpreting social and demographic trends. No one can predict the future, but someone with foresight can perceive the future in the present and make contingency plans or make bets. Leaders with foresight are attuned to changes in technology, public policy, fashions, and customer behavior.

Goran Collert of Swedbank foresaw Sweden's financial crisis in the 1990s. Besides scanning, he regularly checked in with knowledgeable people in Sweden and other countries. This prepared him to restructure the Swedish savings banks.

Steve Jobs showed analytic, practical, and creative intelligence in designing products he correctly predicted would be bought by large numbers of customers. In contrast, the Bell Labs invented a form of mobile telephony[6] and in 1980 asked McKinsey, a consultancy, to predict how many people would be using it in 2000. McKinsey estimated 900,000 and AT&T gave away the invention, buying it back ten years later from McCaw Cellular for $11.5 billion. Unlike the leaders of AT&T, Craig McCaw had the foresight to buy cellular licenses in the early 1980s.

Lack of foresight has damaged companies and lost them opportunities. I was consultant to AT&T's vice president of strategy in 1990 when he sent a memo to top management proposing that the company create a strong Internet capability. He wrote that future shopping would be on the Internet, possibly replacing 800 numbers. The memo came back with "This is Star Wars fantasy" written in the margin, and AT&T lost a great opportunity.

Here are the kind of questions leaders should ask to develop foresight.

EXTERNAL QUESTIONS FOR THE ORGANIZATION

1. What changes are taking place in the markets for our products and services? How will these changes affect our offerings in the future?
2. What changes are taking place in the political and economic environments in which we operate? How will these changes affect the way we operate?
3. What changes in technology could affect our offerings or our processes? For example, in health care, how can technology help the patient with more effective self-care?
4. Will future needs of our customers demand different products and services? Can we observe changes in needs in the population, segmented by age, sex, and income?
5. What changes can we predict in the number and types of our competitors?
6. What changes can we predict in our suppliers and their offerings?
7. What changes are taking place in the environment that will affect our customers and our suppliers?

INTERNAL QUESTIONS FOR THE ORGANIZATION

1. What will be our future offerings?
2. What changes will they require in our organization?
3. What human resources will be required in the future? What skills will we need? What kinds of education and training will we need?
4. What changes will be required in securing capital and other financial resources? Will we be expanding, decentralizing, or centralizing our operations? Will we seek acquisitions?
5. What are we learning from our results and experiences that suggest future needs, opportunities, and challenges?

To develop foresight leaders can:

1. scan the environment by communicating with experts and attending meetings where they present new ideas, reading about new technology, techniques, and legislation;

2. study leading organizations—when I worked with Volvo, I went with a group of managers to visit and study Nissan, Honda, and Toyota. We learned what it would take to reach their levels of quality and productivity;

3. develop scenarios about possible futures and work on contingency plans;

4. join groups of companies that share findings. In health care, Intermountain, Mayo Clinic, Cleveland Clinic, and UCLA Medical Center share effective new medical techniques;

5. serve on the boards of exemplary organizations to learn how they achieve success.

Visioning as Designing the Idealized Organization

Visions are often wishful pictures of greatness, such as becoming "the leading company in our market." These visions sometimes backfire, as when Jack Welch proclaimed that GE companies must become first or second in their markets. Some company executives just shrunk their markets in order to be first or second. Wishful visions do not describe the idealized design of a future organization. In contrast, Ackoff described a strategic vision as a systemic blueprint of an ideal future that would achieve the organization's purpose more effectively and efficiently. Chapter 5 describes Ackoff's approach to designing and implementing a vision. However, committing an organization to a change strategy may face resistance and require courage.

QUESTIONS ON VISIONING

1. Do you have a vision of an ideal organizational future? Or do you have a vision that is a wishful aspiration?

2. Does your vision uniquely position your company in the market?

3. Does it take account of the threats and opportunities for your organization?

4. Will it take courage to commit the organization to change?

Partnering

Partnering is essential within and outside the organization. Leaders need internal partners with complementary skills and style. The leadership team needs all the qualities of strategic intelligence. It's a rare leader who can do it alone. For example, not everyone is good at foresight, but someone on the leadership team should have this ability. However, the ability to develop and sustain productive partnering relationships is an essential quality for leaders to build effective leadership teams and valuable relationships with provider, customer, and supplier organizations. Chapter 6 describes how knowledge of head and heart equips you to choose the right partners.

When executives mentor talented younger employees, the relationship can become a form of partnering. Sheryl Sandberg, who has counseled women to be more self-affirmative at work,[7] owes a part of her success to a mentoring–partnering relationship with Larry Summers when he was Secretary of the Treasury. Sandberg went on to partner successfully as an operations leader with Mark Zuckerberg, FaceBook's strategic leader. In mentoring relationships, younger partners sometimes mentor their elders on using the latest technologies while the older partner mentors on strategy and relationships.

There is a continuum in partnering with suppliers and organizational customers. A comprehensive partnering supplier program guides suppliers from being commodity suppliers who compete on the basis of price and quality against producers of similar products through five levels of partnership arrangements (see Figure 2.3). Value-added suppliers customize a framework agreement to provide a focused service, as FedEx has with the US Postal Service (USPS) to handle airport-to-airport mail delivery, leaving the USPS with the local last-mile

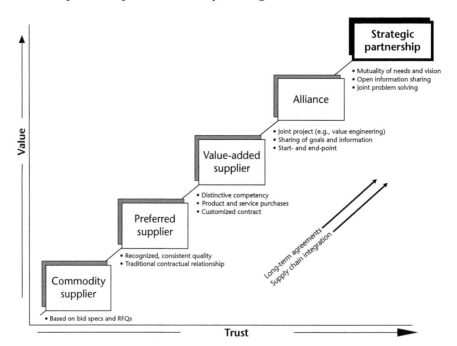

Figure 2.3. Partnering continuum

delivery. Alliance suppliers participate in joint development with the buyer, such as Intel with computer makers like HP. Strategic partners establish a common vision based on mutual needs and strategy, as Northwest Airlines and KLM had for fifteen years under the Wings Alliance before they merged in 2008. The Kaiser Hospital system and Permanente group of physicians is a strategic partnership. When he was CEO, David Lawrence forged a strategic partnership with the Kaiser-Permanente unions. An early example of a partnership in health care is that of the Mayo brothers with the Sisters of St Francis Hospital in 1885.

Companies that form true partnerships collaborate closely with partners to achieve lower total cost, faster speed to market, more innovation, and better quality. The higher the level of partnering, the greater the level of trust required. Good partnering cannot be based on contracts alone. It requires shared values that support a relationship of trust.

INTERNAL QUESTIONS ON PARTNERING

1. Do you know your strengths? If so, do you seek out partners who complement them?
2. Do you know your weaknesses? If so, do you seek out partners who can help you develop and/or compensate for your weaknesses on the leadership team?
3. Do you make sure your internal partners share your leadership philosophy?
4. Do you spell out what you expect from partners?
5. Do you break off ineffective partnering relationships in a timely way?

EXTERNAL QUESTIONS ON PARTNERING

1. Do you partner with key customers to reduce total costs in your joint systems?
2. Do you partner with key suppliers to reduce total costs in your joint systems?
3. Do you build trust with partners by assuring that you share values?
4. Do you make sure that both you and your partners benefit from the partnership?

Engaging and Motivating

We are all motivated by our needs, drives, and values. We are motivated to eat, sleep, relate to others, work, play, and gain information. Our work ties us to a real world that tells us whether or not our ideas make sense, whether or not our skills are valued. Work demands that we discipline our talents and master our impulses. To realize our potential, we must focus our abilities in a way that connects with others, that is valued. We need to feel needed. Our sense of dignity and self-worth depends on being recognized by others through our work. Without work, we deteriorate. We need to work; we need to make a contribution. The challenge for leaders is to engage people's internally driven motivation, the intrinsic motivation to work and contribute. Surveys report that leaders are not very successful at motivating people at work.

Based on polling in 2010–2012, Gallup reports that companies with many employees who are engaged in their work are more successful than those with fewer engaged employees, but only 13 percent of employees worldwide are engaged in their jobs, 24 percent are actively disengaged, and the rest (63 percent) are not engaged. These percentages vary by country. More workers are engaged in the US (30 percent) than Canada (16 percent), UK (17 percent), France (9 percent), Germany (15 percent) or Sweden (16 percent). Managers, executives, and professionals are more engaged than service and manufacturing workers, but a large majority of all categories are not engaged.[8] What is the reason why? Almost everyone wants a job, and everyone is motivated. Why do managers who may be self-motivated fail to engage the intrinsic motivation of the employees they manage?

One answer is that managers neither understand nor know how to engage intrinsic motivation. They believe employees will be motivated by economic incentives, even though there is abundant evidence of the limitations of this type of motivation. Of course, employees will be resentful if they feel they are not fairly paid for their work, and they will be disengaged and alienated if both not paid fairly and given meaningless work. But they will be engaged and motivated only when work is meaningful, connected to their skills and motivational values, and rewarded fairly (see Figure 2.4).[9]

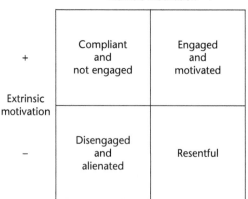

Figure 2.4. Intrinsic/extrinsic motivation

Furthermore, when leaders relate to collaborators with both head and heart, they strengthen a motivating relationship.

QUESTIONS ON ENGAGING AND MOTIVATING

1. Do you know whether people in your organization are engaged and motivated? If so, how do you know?
2. Do you understand what motivates your employees?
3. Do you put people into jobs that engage their intrinsic motivation?
4. Are people in your organization fairly paid for their work?

Chapter 7 will present conceptual tools for engaging and motivating people at work.

Leadership Philosophy

Gallup reports that companies with engaged employees communicated a philosophy and a clear vision; both are elements of strategic intelligence.

Most organizations I have studied or worked with publish a set of values. When managers have responded to a gap survey that asks how important each value is to the organization's success compared to how well the value is practiced, the result shows gaps between importance and practice. In a number of organizations, measurements clash with stated values, as when the value of teamwork is contradicted by measurements of individual performance alone. In these organizations, value statements trigger cynicism, not trust.

A leadership philosophy that is communicated and practiced throughout an organization can create trust and give meaning to work. It helps to define a business and the value it offers to customers. I discuss leadership philosophy in Chapter 4, and give examples of effective leadership philosophies that clarify:

- *Purpose*—the description of the organization's purpose, why it exists, what needs it answers;
- *Practical values*—the behavior essential to achieving that purpose;
- *Ethical and Moral Reasoning* used for decision making;
- *Results*—the definition and measurement of results that reinforce the purpose and values.

Profound Knowledge

Strategic leaders need subject matter knowledge relevant to their industries. They also need profound knowledge, including understanding of systems, variation, and knowledge creation, as well as motivation. This knowledge empowers leaders and collaborators to improve and/or transform an organization. It is not necessary for leaders to be experts in all the elements of profound knowledge. They can partner with colleagues who complement their ability to understand and employ these conceptual tools. However, leaders of change should understand the basic theories in each area and how they interact. The following is a brief description of each area and how it interacts with strategic intelligence.

Understanding Systems

Systems thinking is essential for developing an idealized design of an organization. However, it is the weakest ability in the executives my colleagues and I have interviewed about their strategic intelligence.

The brief definition of a system is: a set of interrelated parts that interact to further the system's purpose. Each part of the system should be evaluated according to how well it interacts with the others to achieve the system's purpose. Ackoff distinguished three types of systems: mechanical systems, like automobiles, that people can design; organic systems, like the human body, that are genetically designed; and social systems, organizations that are made up of processes and people who have purposes of their own.

For a social system to function effectively, people must be made to serve the system's purpose. In a bureaucracy, this is done mechanically, by putting people in rigid roles with strictly stated objectives, coordinated and controlled by a managerial hierarchy. A learning organization is a different type of social system. It is a collection of interdependent processes and other elements with people working interactively, guided by practical values, to accomplish the purpose of the system. For a learning organization to function effectively, people need to be engaged and motivated. They should want to help achieve the organization's purpose. It should be meaningful to them. It follows that only when leadership articulates and practices a philosophy that is meaningful to people will a learning organization be effective.

A weakness of many bureaucracies is that some of the parts, divisions, and projects do not interact to further the organization's purpose. Parts are evaluated individually, not systemically. Companies may boast of great marketing or HR departments that do not interact, like great automotive engines that are not designed to fit the other parts of the car. When HP acquired Compaq, managers were told to choose the best practices from each company to design the merged organization. One of the managers assigned to this project told me that this resulted in a mess, processes that did not interact, a busted bureaucracy.

Finally, it is important to understand that a system should be designed to adapt to a larger system. Cars are designed differently to function well on mountain roads versus super highways, and where petroleum is expensive versus where it is relatively cheap. So, too, organizations should be designed to fit different markets and cultures. An organization that produces commodity products and services will be different from one that interacts with business customers to solve problems.

The challenge for leaders of organizational change is to:

1. partner with their teams to design the organizations essential to achieve their purpose. These may be ambidextrous organizations. These organizations should be able to gain and retain customers while continually increasing quality and cutting costs;

2. design a structure of roles and processes that makes it easy for people to collaborate to implement an idealized design;

3. articulate a leadership philosophy with purpose and values that engages people who come to work with their own purposes.

In Chapter 5, we expand the discussion of systems thinking and its relationship to visioning.

Understanding Variation

Organizational leaders are bombarded with information. To understand the meaning of information, they need knowledge of variation and statistics. To improve processes, employees throughout organizations need to understand variation, otherwise empowerment will be a license to tamper with the organization.

Leaders are constantly faced with variation and the need to make decisions based on how variation is interpreted and understood. Does a drop in sales indicate a pattern? Was improved performance the result of changes we made, or was it just luck? When data is plotted over time, the patterns may or may not allow predictions that the pattern will continue. To determine the difference, it is necessary to distinguish *common causes* and *special causes*. *Common causes* affect all outcomes of the process and act on everyone working in the process. To change an outcome due to a common cause, you must redesign the process. *Special causes* are not part of a process and do not occur all the time or affect everyone. To deal with a special cause, you do not have to redesign the process.

When common causes alone affect the outcomes, a process is *stable* or in a state of *statistical control*. Variations in outcomes are predictable within set limits. When outcomes are affected by both common and special causes of variation, the process is *unstable*. This does not necessarily mean that there are large variations in outcome, but that variations are unpredictable. If special causes are identified and removed, the process becomes stable and performance becomes predictable. An unstable process can be improved by identifying the special causes, taking appropriate action, then continuing to plot the data over time to determine that the changes have improved the process.

Knowledge of statistics also empowers leaders to question the significance of findings from experiments and studies. Leaders should be skeptical of findings that do not follow good statistical practice, such as randomization of a universe tested. They should question results based on correlations, since a correlation does not prove cause and affect. They should question "significant" findings that explain a small part of the variance.

A leader's decisions are often based on statistical evidence. By understanding variation and statistics, leaders are empowered to make better decisions.

Understanding Motivation

Both partnering and motivating require understanding yourself and the people you work with and lead. Understanding people means understanding what motivates them and how they interact with each other. This understanding helps leaders to predict how people will respond to their initiatives, why they embrace or resist change, and what it takes to engage them in collaboration.

We all have the tendency to view our own behavior as a rational response to a situation, while viewing the behavior of others as expressing their personalities. However, we all have values and motives that interact with our interpretation of a situation. Chapter 6 describes the elements of personality.

Personality types can help us predict behavior, but they do not equip a leader to understand emotions. To understand that people are anxious or angry, hopeful or despairing requires a heart that listens. How to develop both conceptual and emotional understanding to engage and motivate people is discussed in Chapter 7.

Understanding the Creation of Knowledge

Strategy requires prediction and learning from experience. By developing theories and testing hypotheses, strategists can create knowledge. Effective strategists establish a common purpose and practical values, but allow freedom of action to innovate, to develop new knowledge. However, new knowledge and practice will be most useful when it furthers an organization's purpose and reflects its values.

There are different ways of creating knowledge. Leaders with foresight develop theories based on patterns of data and behavior they observe. These theories can be tested by strategic decisions. People in all parts of an organization can test theories to improve processes and practice. Some theories can be tested by controlled experiments. Deming recommended using the Shewart cycle of plan–do–study–act (PDSA) to test theories of improvement. At AT&T, we determined that any changes should be positive for customers, employees, and owners.

Developing new knowledge at work can be an interactive process. A theory leads to a hypothesis and predictions of results. When the results don't confirm the hypothesis, the discrepancy of data to theory can stimulate a modification of the hypothesis and a new test. Or it can cause a person to rethink the theory.

However, the ability to innovate, to develop knowledge, depends on attitudes and values. As Daniel Kahneman points out, contrary to the rules of philosophers of science who advise testing hypothesis by trying to refute them, people (and scientists quite often) seek data that are likely to be compatible with the beliefs they already hold."[10] This is called *confirmatory bias*.

Management groups often hold on to faulty theories. When I was consulting to a management team of a Finnish company that sold fish feed to salmon farmers in Norway, the managers assumed they were losing business because of price competition. I urged them to interview the farmers and ask what was most valuable to them. At first, they resisted, claiming they knew from experience what the farmers wanted. I persisted, and they agreed to humor me. The next time we met, they reported, with embarrassment, that the farmers told them that feed affects the color of the salmon. Some customers want red salmon filets and others want a pale color. Subsequently, they customized the fish feed and improved sales. I have found this same reluctance of managers to test their theories by interviewing customers in other companies. Every time I have succeeded in getting senior managers to interview key customers, the results has been to improve their theories and practice.

National cultures can also make a difference. In Sweden, management groups highly value consensus and managers sometimes withhold ideas that might cause conflict. In Germany, leaders encourage colleagues to criticize theories and practice, as long as they can present supporting data.

In many organizations, knowledge is lost because mistakes are punished, not studied as opportunities for improvement of people and processes. When they are studied, it is often found that the process was at fault. Deming referred to the *attribution error*, attributing a mistake to a person rather than a process, a special rather than a common cause.

Employing Strategic Intelligence

There is no standard pathway or formula for change. Rather, the qualities of strategic intelligence equip you to choose and follow a path to effective change. There is logic to starting with a clear purpose and philosophy. The reasons for change generally have to do with adapting to threats or exploiting opportunities and innovations. A leadership team needs to develop a vision and motivate the organization, but there is no one best way to do this. It may combine top-down, bottom-up, and interactive initiatives.

In summary, strategic intelligence is a system of qualities of mind and heart that equip leaders with the conceptual tools essential to creating a better future for an organization. The Appendix includes a Strategic Intelligence Inventory to evaluate and develop your strategic intelligence. But even with strategic intelligence, strategic decisions require good judgment and courage. Sometimes information is inadequate. Leaders may be uncertain about an investment, or they may have doubts about selecting other leaders. However, with strategic intelligence, their judgment will be strengthened.

Notes

1. Michael E. Porter, *Competitive Advantage, Creating and Sustaining Superior Performance* (New York: The Free Press, 1985).
2. Robert J. Sternberg, *Beyond IQ: A Triarchic Theory of Human Intelligence* (New York: Cambridge University Press, 1993).
3. As a result of King Solomon's asking God for a heart that listens, "all the world courted him to hear the wisdom that God had put in his heart" (I: Kings 10:24: New English Bible).
4. Ibn Khaldûn, *The Muqaddimah*, trans. Franz Rosenthal, Bollingen Series XLIII (Princeton, NJ: Princeton University Press, 1958).
5. Antonio Damasio, *Descartes' Error: Emotion, Reason, and the Human Brain* (New York: Penguin Books, 1994), p. xii.
6. Ericsson introduced the world's first fully automatic mobile telephone system, MTA, in 1956.
7. Sheryl Sandberg, *Lean In* (New York: Alfred A. Knopf, 2013).
8. Gallup, Inc., *The State of the Global Workplace: Employee Engagement for Business Leaders Worldwide* (Gallup, 2014), at: <http://www.gallup.com/services/178517/state-global-workplace.aspx> (accessed December 2014). Gallup measures employee engagement based on workers' responses to its Q^{12} survey, which consists of 12 actionable workplace elements with proven links to performance outcomes. To identify these elements, Gallup spent years conducting thousands of interviews at every level of various organizations, in most industries, and in several countries. Since Gallup finalized the Q^{12} question wording in the late 1990s, the survey has

been administered to more then 25 million employees in 189 different countries and 69 languages. For a listing of the Q^{12} survey items and more information on how they relate to business performance outcome, see the full State of the Global Workplace report.

9. See, for example, Edward L Deci with Richard Flaste, *Why We Do What We Do: Understanding Self Motivation* (New York: Penguin Books, 1995).

10. Daniel Kahneman. *Thinking Fast and Slow* (New York: Farrar, Straus and Giroux, 2011), p. 81.

3

Leadership for Change

Leadership is the art of getting someone else to do something you want done because he wants to do it, not because your position of power can compel him to do it.

—Dwight D. Eisenhower

Steve Jobs of Apple and Sam Palmisano of IBM were two of the greatest business leaders of the early twenty-first century. Both had the foresight to exploit opportunities and lead change. Both were visionaries, Jobs in terms of creating "insanely great" new products, Palmisano in terms of wrapping products in solutions. Both were able to motivate collaboration and get people to want to do what they needed done. Both demonstrated strategic intelligence. But their personalities and methods were different. Jobs led what he called "deep collaboration" by combining the fear of failure with the promise of greatness. Palmisano engaged thousands of IBMers in identifying the values essential to developing a collaborative culture where teams of different specialists could work together with business and government customers.

Leadership is a word and a concept that has been more argued than almost any other I know.

—Dwight D. Eisenhower

One reason that leadership is a word and concept that has been argued so much is that there are different kinds of leaders in terms of personality, role, and behavior. A definition may fit one type but not others. Another reason has to do with the definition of good leadership. The word "good" can mean either effectively good or morally good. Leaders can be effective but morally bad when, like Adolf Hitler and Josef Stalin, their purpose is control, conquest, and destruction. Effective and morally good leaders, like Abraham Lincoln and Nelson Mandela, inspire collaboration for the common good, for a higher moral purpose. They stimulate and support independence, dialogue, and responsibility rather than conformity, tribalism, and exploitation.

Of all the definitions proposed, the one definition of a leader that seems to me unarguable is: *a leader is someone with followers*. If you have followers, you are a leader, and if you do not have followers, you are not a leader, even if you have a formal position of authority. Leadership, then, is a relationship between leaders and followers. But this relationship has varied in different cultures and organizations. In some contexts, the leadership model has been autocratic. In other contexts, it has been collaborative.

Leaders of change in the age of knowledge work are different from autocratic or bureaucratic leaders. They need collaborators, who *want* to collaborate and innovate. To gain collaboration, leaders may have to change how people think as well as what they do. They may need to encourage the doubters, infuse the belief that people can change an organization's future and provide the tools to make it happen. No leader of a complex organization can do this alone. Leadership of change in the age of knowledge work and learning organizations requires different types of leaders working together.

In contrast to leadership, management has to do with administering processes and control systems, like planning, budgeting, evaluating, and measuring. It has to do with completing tasks rather than engaging followers. Managers can share their responsibilities or hand them off to others. Most tasks and responsibilities of management can be delegated to teams, like those in the Morningstar Company in California, where employees are self-managed.[1] *The Economist* reports that some companies have begun delegating management functions to machines.[2]

In the past, managers usually knew their subordinates' jobs better then they did. In knowledge organizations, where many subordinates are experts who know more about their job than do their bosses, managers need leadership skills to develop collaborative teams. In some large companies, team members are located in different places. Management needs to be shared, and leadership requires exceptional communication skills.

In contrast to management, leadership is a relationship that can't be given away. If people follow you because they want to follow you, you cannot hand over that relationship to someone else. To achieve positive change, organizations need both management and leadership, but they don't necessarily need managers.

The Context of Leadership

Leadership depends not only on qualities like strategic intelligence, but also on context. In one context, someone may be a leader and not so in another context. It's a mistake to describe the qualities needed for leadership without indicating the context. The context for leadership includes two main factors:

1. the challenges facing a leader;
2. the values and attitudes of followers.

Like other primates, we have a tendency to form hierarchies because of our drive for mastery, which can become a drive for power over others. But to satisfy our need for dignity, we prefer egalitarian organizations. We recognize that leadership may be needed and we sometimes idealize leaders for a while, especially when they appear to be helping us respond to a challenge. As my study of Swedish leadership showed, idealization can turn to contempt when people decide a leader is no longer useful, or has even become a danger to them.

In tribes of hunter-gatherers, leaders were needed for hunting and war parties, but once the action was over, they were not allowed to hold on to authority. If they tried to retain command, they were ridiculed, shamed, and even ostracized.[3] In normal times, peasant villagers see no need for leaders. The family is an independent unit that resists outside interference. There is little need for change. In the Mexican village that Erich Fromm and I studied, villagers would decide together to take on a project like improving a road or building a schoolhouse. However, when they were threatened by government troops during the revolution of 1910–20, the peasants of this and other villages in Morelos, Mexico needed a leader, and they recruited Emiliano Zapata to defend them.

Some worker-owned cooperative organizations don't need leaders. Like peasant villages, decisions can be made by committees of owner-workers.[4] In the open-source software community of hackers who develop Linux and Apache systems, unpaid project leaders emerge to decide on features, when to release software, and when to pass on the baton. It's a more modern version of a hunter-gatherer community.[5]

Leadership qualities that serve in one context may not in another. In the 1980s, managers and administrators, not leaders, ran AT&T and the government agencies with which I worked. These bureaucracies were governed by rules and regulations, designed to keep things moving on a predictable path.

In these bureaucracies, leaders were rare and viewed with suspicion, because they questioned policies and recruited followers who became disruptive insurgents. At AT&T, a visionary leader in the ranks of middle management kept provoking top management by questioning practices until he was allowed to lead a spin-off company. In government agencies, the few entrepreneurial leaders I met became frustrated by the bureaucracy and left for the private sector.

Some entrepreneurs who were not trusted by bureaucracies in both the public and private sectors created new companies in the 1990s. However, an entrepreneur may lead a pioneering group to create an enterprise, but fail to be effective in leading an established company that requires a different kind of leadership. Many entrepreneurial leaders have the type of personality I have termed productive narcissist.[6] They are visionaries who want to change the world and whose success convinces them that they don't have to listen to the doubters or naysayers.

In Silicon Valley in the 1980s and 1990s, corporate boards sometimes replaced visionary entrepreneurs with what they called "adult supervision," more conservative managerial types.[7] This was not always successful. In 1985, the Apple board replaced Jobs—whose dictatorial arrogance was alienating the organization—with John Sculley, who had been CEO of Pepsi. It was a disaster. Sculley was a marketing manager and Apple needed a leader to create innovative products. When Jobs returned as CEO in 1997, he had improved his strategic intelligence by learning to partner with leaders who complemented his creativity and vision: Tim Cook in operations and Jony Ives in design.

The Changing Mode of Production

The challenges facing a leader are different, depending on the kind of organization and the leader's role. A major challenge of our time is adapting to the new mode of production of knowledge work and leading change from bureaucracies to collaborative learning organizations.

One-hundred-and-fifty years ago, most employment in the Western world was on farms or in craft workshops. The twentieth century was dominated by a transition to industrial and related service work, and now most people in these countries are working at service jobs (over 70 percent in Germany and 80 percent in the US and the UK). Some of these jobs require little education or training: waiters, room cleaners in hotels, security guards, janitors, street cleaners, etc. Their work does not change much and can be supervised by managers who are not leaders. But other jobs require knowledge, collaboration, and the ability to keep learning.

The change from industrial work to knowledge work requires a change in the mode of production, the way work is organized, the tools used, and the skills and relationships required for effectiveness and efficiency. I've termed it *technoservice*.[8] The change from farming-craft work to industrial work also meant a change in the mode of production from individuals or small groups using hand tools to bureaucracies of workers using electromechanical tools in jobs formatted in a hierarchy of roles. Although many service businesses, such as fast-food restaurants and retail stores, are organized as industrial bureaucracies, knowledge organizations using advanced technology need collaborative teams and collaborative leaders to:

- create innovative offerings;
- work across organizational silos;
- work with suppliers, customers, and clients to solve business or health problems;
- work across national cultures.

Even in ambidextrous manufacturing companies like the automotive industry, collaborative teams speed up the process from design to production. Much of today's agricultural industry no longer uses the tools of the peasant farmer. Work requires the knowledge mode of production, using biotechnology to modify crops and increase production. In the most effective medical centers, teams of doctors, nurses, and other providers collaborate to solve complex problems and continuously improve processes.[9] Business and government customers increasingly ask suppliers for solutions rather than products, requiring collaboration that moves up the partnering continuum shown in Chapter 2. Even the military, facing new kinds of enemies, needs to change. General David Petraeus has stated that the army has been too bureaucratic to succeed against insurgents. He has written, "learning organizations defeat insurgencies, bureaucratic hierarchies do not."[10] Other US military thinkers have expanded the reasons for change and emphasized the need for leaders of change. Dean Anderson and Linda Ackerman Anderson write:

> Both the Chairman of the Joint Chiefs of Staff and the Supreme Allied Commander of Allied Command Transformation of the North Atlantic Treaty Organization have called for globally integrated operations and interoperability, greater agility and versatility, collaborative relationships across Forces and with Allies and partners, technical advancements, and leveraged shared resources . . . These are the right strategies; however, having military leaders prepared to perform well in these new ways of operating, when they require leadership that is so different from historical leadership and organizational practices, will require advanced and sustained development, starting now.[11]

Leading Change in Knowledge Work

To build learning organizations, leaders of change are needed throughout an organization, not just at the top. Strategic leaders assess the forces shaping the market and lead a team in deciding about offerings, acquisitions, and partnering and designing a vision of how the organization can succeed in the future. Partnering with operational managers, they develop a change strategy, and operational managers throughout the organization construct processes needed to implement the vision. Together with network leaders, they form and facilitate the teams and projects that make it happen.[12] All of these leaders need to engage, empower, and motivate a diverse staff to collaborate and continually improve the processes that shape the desired future. To do this, these leaders need to build trust between each other. They need to be able to use dialogue and debate based on facts and reasoning to improve decision making, and to avoid interpersonal conflict. They need to respect differences in their styles and competencies. They need to understand people as well as business. Leadership needs to become a creative partnership among three different types of leaders with different skills and personalities:

- Strategic;
- Operational;
- Network.

Strategic leaders define purpose, vision, and practical values. They make sure that products and processes are aligned with purpose and practical values. They educate an organization about the reasons for change. The most effective strategic leaders partner with others so that the leadership team has all the qualities of strategic intelligence.

Strategic leaders recognize that change stirs up resistance, and they have different approaches for getting everyone on board. Some are like Jeff Bezos of Amazon, who encourages "arguments backed by numbers and passions."[13] Some are like Jobs, who was quick to fire resisters. And others are like Palmisano, who used training and incentives to overcome resistance. Chapter 7 presents tools that leaders can use to turn resistance into collaboration.

How strategic leaders lead change depends on their personality. Palmisano, with an adaptive personality, was respectfully interactive with subordinates and customers. Leaders like Jobs and Bezos—the narcissistic visionaries intent on changing the world—are aggressive, extremely competitive, and see subordinates as human resources, to be used as long as they are useful. They are not easy to work for. When displeased, their angry put-downs can be cruel. In his biography of Bezos, Brad Stone cites some of these, such as "Are you lazy or just incompetent?"[14] Similar put-downs have been reported by victims of Jobs, Bill Gates, and other strategic leaders. Yet, despite their fear, subordinates stay on because of the challenge, pride in being part of a great enterprise, and the promise of wealth.

Sidney Harman, the visionary CEO who sponsored the Bolivar Project and led change at Harman Industries and the University of Southern California (USC) was another strategic leader with a narcissistic personality. He demonstrated strategic intelligence by foresight in developing the high-fidelity industry and visioning a more humane and productive organization. I asked him to describe what he did as a leader, and he emphasized his role in supporting innovation, educating managers, and inspiring the workforce. He went on to say that he did this by promoting "value driven competence, communicating what I believe in and developing the skills necessary to implement these values." The values included product excellence, innovation, and respect for diversity.

Like many effective strategic leaders, Harman combined business skills with an aesthetic sense, expressed not only in products but also in the expression of his values. He believed that technology combined with the arts led to innovation, and he instituted a program at the University of Southern California that combines technology and the arts.

Harman also described his role in making strategic decisions. He said he "rejected the reckless and embraced the daring." He was proud of his ability to close a win–win deal. He confessed that he sometimes could not control his anger at subordinates who questioned his ideas and decisions without supporting evidence or reasoned argument, but by saying "It doesn't feel right" or "It can't be done." Like Jobs and Bezos, Harman got many things done that subordinates thought were impossible to achieve.

Harman's lieutenants admitted to being afraid of his anger, and sometimes holding back on reporting problems or bad news. However, they said that Harman inspired and energized the company. So did Jobs and so does Bezos.

Operational leaders are in charge of designing and maintaining the processes that implement a vision. They may lead teams and projects at all levels of an organization. Some of these are essential for continually improving production and supply-chain logistics. Jeff Wilke of Amazon led operations to create huge fulfillment centers (FCs). Just as Cook partnered with Jobs, Wilke implemented the processes needed to implement Bezo's vision. A supply chain vice president told Brad Stone, "They fed off each other. Bezos wanted to do it and Wilke knew how to do it."[15] Operational leaders head improvement processes that are ongoing in all parts of a learning organization. They lead meetings to analyze performance data to learn from each unit's efforts to meet goals and improve performance.[16] Change never ends for them.

Some of the most effective operational leaders have exacting personalities. They are good at finding ways to cut costs and improve processes. But like Mark Hurd, who became CEO of HP, they tend to sacrifice innovation for efficiency. Hurd was not a strategic leader. When he left HP, the company lacked new products. Working with Larry Ellison of Oracle, who is a visionary strategist, Hurd's operational competence has been put to good use.

I have worked with operational leaders in middle management who have been able to engage subordinates and union reps in projects to improve processes. They did so by articulating and practicing values that responded to the needs of customers and employees, as well as owners. They gained trust by teaching teams to take over some of the management functions and trusting them to carry them out. They drove out fear by treating mistakes as opportunities for learning and improving processes. They made it harder to make mistakes and easier to do things right.

The weakness of some operational leaders with obsessive personalities is over-control and micro-management. They do not get the benefit of trusting others. People follow them because they have to, not because they want to. Subordinates follow orders but fear to step out of the box.

Network leaders are needed by knowledge organizations that provide complex solutions for their customers. They connect experts across disciplines, organizational departments, and regions. To do this, they must develop the trust and facilitate the communication to make experts from different disciplines and departments collaborate. An excellent example was Lou Viraldi of Ford, who in 1980 facilitated groups of designers and engineers who produced the Ford Taurus, a car that lifted the company from near bankruptcy. Usually, Ford designers would send a design to product engineers, who would criticize it and send it back for redesign until they agreed to send it to the production engineers, who would criticize it in terms of cost and would send it back, and so on for a number of years. By bringing representatives of these three groups together and also stimulating ideas from the shop floor, Viraldi led Ford experts in concurrent engineering that cut the time and cost to produce a best-selling car. In this process, operational leadership became heterarchical, shifting to the person who was the expert in each phase of the project.

At the Mayo Clinic and other Mayo-type healthcare organizations, such as the Geisinger, Cleveland, and Hitchcock clinics, some physicians are network leaders who take charge of a patient and make sure all specialists work together on the case. IBM trains network leaders who form teams of consultants, hardware, and software experts to solve the problems of business and government customers. Ideally, operational leaders also have qualities of network leaders. However, network leaders are most effective when they do not have a hierarchical position but are able to facilitate collaboration because they are trusted for their impartiality, judgment, and understanding of people. They succeed because people want to collaborate with them. As Jay Galbraith points out, a would-be network leader without these qualities will not succeed.[17]

I have been a network leader, facilitating agreement in different contexts: union and management, top leadership teams, managers from different countries, the National Coalition on Health Care. In none of these contexts did I have any authority other than what the participants granted. However, I worked together with strategic and operational leaders to understand organizational strategy and what was needed to implement it.

To lead change successfully, strategic, operational, and network leaders need to become an interactive leadership team with strategic intelligence (see Figure 3.1). My colleagues and I have helped develop this kind of team in workshops using exercises such as you will find in these chapters.

43

Figure 3.1. Integration of the three types of leaders into a leadership team

The Attitudes of Followers

Leadership effectiveness also depends on the attitudes of followers. Chapter 6 describes changes in the social character in the highly industrialized societies, caused by changes in families, technology, and work. The kind of personality shaped in families with sole, male wage earners fit smoothly into male-dominated bureaucracies led by paternalistic administrators. The men and very few women moving up the bureaucratic hierarchy transferred on to their bosses their childhood images of a good father. However, this idealization kept them from fully growing up and affirming their own views at work.

The kind of personality shaped in families with dual or single female wage earners reacts against paternalism and responds to collaborative leadership. Rather than presenting themselves as larger-than-life and omniscient, leaders will engage these men and women by articulating and practicing an organizational philosophy that they find meaningful. We will return to this in Chapter 7.

National cultures also influence attitudes to leadership. Japan adopted the Chinese Confucian model of leadership that emphasizes teaching, mentoring, cooperation, and mutual obligation.[18] The Western ideal is the individual entrepreneur, the hero, who creates a cult-like company, or alternatively a military leader who commands an army. Much of the leadership training in the West aims at humanizing individualistic leaders. This training can be useful, but it misses the point that to develop collaborative learning organizations different types of leadership should be developed with the qualities of strategic intelligence.

Leading Change

In any context, strategic, operational, and network leaders need to interact to develop a shared purpose and the products, practical values, and processes necessary to achieve that purpose. As we discuss in Chapter 5, purpose, products, practical values, people (roles and skills), and processes need to be developed as a system. These Five Ps become the organization's vision that will be worked on at all levels and parts of the organization. By working on implementing the vision, everyone comes to understand it.

Ideally, strategic CEOs will lead change together with key operational leaders. They will avoid the temptation to wall themselves off from a workforce that wants to know what they believe and wants to relate to them. A study of the best-performing academic medical centers in the US reported that when the CEOs together with the chairs led the change process and accepted personal responsibility for quality and safety results, quality improved and there were fewer deaths caused by avoidable mistakes.[19]

Although it is essential that a CEO strongly support change, some CEO strategists who are not good at leading a change process delegate that role to operational leaders. In my experience with change, CEOs have led strategy meetings, but in most cases, operational leaders have led the projects that implemented the vision. At AT&T, some of the vice presidents in charge of large divisions, many larger than most companies, directly led change. The vice presidents led meetings of key managers, and sometimes with union officials, that shaped a vision for the division and the practical values essential to achieve it. Operational leaders then organized change projects in different offices. Change had to measurably benefit customers, employees, and owners. This was pictured as follows (see Figure 3.2).

Customer Value Added (CVA) describes the qualities such as price and technical excellence that make the customers buy AT&T's products rather than those of competitors. Economic Value Added (EVA) based on revenues allows the company to pay dividends to share owners and invest in technology and employees (pay, benefits, training), People Value Added (PVA), whose competence and motivated service produces customer value added.

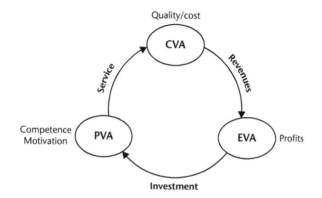

Figure 3.2. Creating value

The change process I helped lead at George Washington University starting in 2000 was presided over by the president, Stephen J. Trachtenberg, but was led by the academic and business executive vice presidents, Donald Lehman and Lou Katz. The EVPs organized separate teams of department chairs and administrators to review results of surveying faculty, students, staff, and parents on the changes they wanted. Their recommendations were integrated into a strategic plan by the executive team, led by the president. Changes were made throughout the university, notably greater emphasis on preparing undergraduates for the global economy by emphasizing language training, critical analysis, and writing skills. Administrators responded to student and parental wishes, such as simplifying interactions with the bursary and improving the mail service.

Any large change process has to integrate executive leadership with unit-level implementation of a strategy. How a vision is developed and implemented will vary, but ideally executives will allow unit leaders freedom to innovate. This will work only if the executive team has communicated the kind of leadership philosophy described in Chapter 4 that serves to evaluate purposed changes and unit leaders develop the ability to create collaborators.

Ronald Heifetz and Marty Linsky offer the metaphor of top leadership setting a strategy for change and watching from a balcony as the people of the organization dance to the melody. They advise the leaders to "move back and forth between the dance floor and the balcony, making interventions, observing their impact in real time and then returning to the action."[20] Heifetz and Linsky in this and other books offer useful advice on leading an organization to adapt to challenges, but their dance of change would be enriched with choreography that includes processes toward a vision and a melody that expresses the purpose and values that direct change. To change a frozen bureaucracy into a learning organization, strategic leaders can observe from a balcony and make brief visits to the dance floor, but operational and network leaders will be on the dance floor most of the time, designing and implementing the choreography, innovative steps that interact to make the dance a work of art rather than a collection of individual dances.

No one dances in a bureaucracy; they stay in line and march to the beat of a drum. Leaders don't need to understand the personalities of followers, because there is little interaction with them. Each person has a clear role and objectives. If they meet their objectives, they will be rewarded. If they do not, they won't be promoted or get a bonus, and they risk being fired.

Bureaucracies don't need leaders with strategic intelligence. Learning organizations do. In a learning organization, everyone dances to the same music, but like a good jazz ensemble or a ballet, there is opportunity for variations on a theme. As described in Chapter 4, the music score is the organization's philosophy. Understanding people is also essential for developing collaboration at all levels. Partnering requires trust based on people understanding each other's strengths. Engaging intrinsic motivation requires understanding personality and placing people in roles where their abilities and personality fit and they can continually develop themselves. Chapter 6 presents conceptual tools for understanding leaders and followers and their relationship.

Questions on Leadership

1. What are your leadership responsibilities?

2. What are the challenges you face?

3. Is your organization trying to become a learning organization? Why, or why not?

4. Does your organization have strategic, operational, and network leadership? If no, what is missing? What can be done to develop this kind of leadership?

5. What type of leader are you or what type do you aspire to become? What can you do to strengthen yourself as a leader?

6. Why would anyone follow you?

Notes

1. Doug Kirkpatrick, *Beyond Empowerment, The Age of the Self-managed Organization* (Morning Star Self-Management Institute, 2011).
2. Schumpeter, "Over the Horizon: Three Issues that Should Preoccupy Managers in the Next 50 Years," *The Economist* (6 September 2014), at: <http://www.economist.com/news/business/21615586-three-issues-should-preoccupy-managers-next-50-years-over-horizon> (accessed December 2014).
3. Christopher Boehm, *Hierarchy in the Forest, The Evolution of Egalitarian Behavior* (Cambridge, MA: Harvard University Press, 1995). Boehm presents evidence that both egalitarianism and hierarchy are innate human traits.
4. See Shaila Dewan, "Who Needs a Boss?," *New York Times*, 25 March 2014, at: <http://www.nytimes.com/2014/03/30/magazine/who-needs-a-boss.html?_r=0> (accessed November 2014).
5. Gianluci Bosco, *Implicit Theories of "Good Leadership" in the Open-source Community*, MA thesis in economy and business administration, Department of Manufacturing, Engineering and Management, Technical University of Denmark, May 2004.
6. Michael Maccoby, *Narcissistic Leaders, Who Succeeds and Who Fails* (Boston, MA: Harvard Business School Press, 2007).
7. See Brad Stone, *The Everything Store, Jeff Bezos and the Age of Amazon* (New York: Little Brown, 2013), p. 98.

8. Michael Maccoby, *Why Work?* (New York: Simon & Schuster, 1988).

9. Michael Maccoby, Clifford L. Norman, Jane Norman, and Richard Margolies, *Transforming Health Care Leadership: A Systems Guide to Improve Patient Care, Decrease Costs, and Improve Population Health* (San Francisco, CA: Jossey Bass, 2013).

10. General David H. Petraeus, USA and Lt General Jams F. Amos, USMC, Foreword to *The U.S. Army—Marine Corps Counterinsurgency Field Manual* (Washington DC: Signalman Publishing, 2009), p. xi.

11. Dean Anderson and Linda Ackerman Anderson, "Leadership Breakthrough: Meeting the Transformational Challenges of 21st Century Security Environment," in Linton Wells II, Theodore C. Halles, and Michael C. Davies (eds), *Changing Mindsets to Transform Security*, edited by Linton Wells II, et al. (Washington DC: Center for Technology and National Security Policy, Institute for National Strategic Studies, National Defense University, 2013), p. 25.

12. Michael Maccoby, *The Leader: A New Face for American Management* (New York: Simon & Schuster, 1981).

13. Brad Stone, *The Everything Store, Jeff Bezos and the Age of Amazon* (New York: Little Brown, 2013), p. 328. One of Amazon's fourteen leadership principles is "Have Backbone, Disagree and Commit."

14. Brad Stone, *The Everything Store, Jeff Bezos and the Age of Amazon* (New York: Little Brown, 2013), p. 177.

15. Brad Stone, *The Everything Store, Jeff Bezos and the Age of Amazon* (New York: Little Brown, 2013), p. 161.

16. For examples of good operational leadership practice, see the work of Robert D. Behn of Harvard's Kennedy School on public service leadership and the examples in Michael Maccoby, Clifford L. Norman, Jane Norman, and Richard Margolies, *Transforming Health Care Leadership: A Systems Guide to Improve Patient Care, Decrease Costs, and Improve Population Health* (San Francisco, CA: Jossey Bass, 2013).

17. Jay R. Galbraith, "Mastering the Law of Requisite Variety with Differentiated Networks," in Charles Heckscher and Paul S. Adler (eds), *The Firm as a Collaborative Community* (Oxford: Oxford University Press, 2006), pp. 179–98.

18. A description of the origin of Chinese leadership philosophy can be found in Arthur Waley, *Three Ways of Thought in Ancient China* (Abingdon, Oxfordshire: Routledge, 2005 [1939]).

19. Mark A. Keroack, B. J. Youngerg, J. L. Cerese, et al., "Organizational Factors Associated with High Performance in Quality and Safety in Academic Medical Centers," *Academic Medicine* 82(12) (2007): 1178–86.

20. Ronald A. Heifetz and Marty Linsky, *Leadership on the Line* (Boston, MA: Harvard Business School Press, 2002), p. 53.

4

Leadership Philosophy: An Essential Tool for Change

We think that for a general about to fight an enemy, it is important to know the enemy's numbers, but still more important to know the enemy's philosophy.

—G. K. Chesterton, cited by William James, *Pragmatism*

Making high profits is the means to the end of fulfilling Whole Foods' core business mission. We want to improve the health and well-being of everyone on the planet through higher-quality food and better nutrition, and we can't fulfill this mission unless we are highly profitable. Just as people cannot live without eating, so a business cannot live without profits. But, most people don't live to eat, and neither must businesses live just to make profits.

—John Mackey, Co-CEO Whole Foods, *Conscious Capitalism*

Effective leaders of change communicate and practice a philosophy that shapes organizational culture and determines how decisions are made about products, people, processes, customers, and communities. As noted in Chapter 2, a leadership philosophy should define the purpose of an organization, the values essential to achieve that purpose, and the way results will be measured. An organizational philosophy is essential for building trust internally and with customers. It invites everyone in the organization to challenge decisions and practices that clash with the values that support the organization's purpose. It provides guidelines for innovation at all levels. It defines the reasons and relationships that inspire enthusiastic engagement and collaboration. It is a necessary tool for positive change (see Figure 4.1).

Bureaucratic organizations are held together by a rigid structure and material incentives. Each person works in a box with defined objectives, coordinated and controlled by someone in the box above. Knowledge organizations are held together by trust. Rather than staying in their boxes, people move out to collaborate across organizational boundaries. Their roles require flexibility, since their objectives may be solutions rather than fixed outputs.

Figure 4.1. Strategic intelligence: focus on leadership philosophy

Coordination and control is shared within groups of people with diverse expertise. Motivation depends on all the Five Rs described in Chapter 7, which are shaped in large part by the organization's philosophy. Reasons for doing the work; responsibilities for tasks and challenges; recognition; rewards; and relationships with colleagues and customers.

Without trust, people in organizations work for themselves, not for the organization and its stakeholders. I learned that by coaching managers termed "high potential" in a large technology company. One manager told me in confidence that he was getting himself transferred from a multi-million-dollar project because he was sure it would fail. I asked if he had reported his view to the team leader so that the project could be stopped and money saved. No, he said, that would make an enemy. It was better for his career just to leave the project.

When people in an organization trust each other, things get done more quickly and easily. People are more open with each other. They share information. To build trust, leaders do the following:

- They communicate a philosophy and practice the values.
- They follow through. They do what they promise.
- They explain what they won't do and why they won't do it.

- They don't blame people for mistakes, but create a dialogue about the reasons for the mistake and what can be done to avoid future mistakes.

- They listen and act on what they hear. They institute processes to facilitate ideas, and they recognize contributions from others; they give credit.

- They work at understanding the people they lead.

The HP Way as Organization Philosophy

When I first studied technology companies in the 1970s, I found Hewlett-Packard (HP) to be unique in developing a collaborative culture. It was based on the philosophy of its founders. I interviewed Bill Hewlett and asked about the purpose of HP. He said it was to make products that were valuable to technical people, because they helped technicians perform better. He went on to describe the organizational values that supported this purpose. They included the following:

- Technical excellence—HP's product developers and production engineers were expected to keep learning so that their knowledge would keep pace with the state of the art in their fields. The company paid their tuition to take courses at the Stanford School of Engineering.

- Collaboration with customers and across disciplines—product development engineers visited customers and talked with them about tools that would help them perform better. On his return to Palo Alto, a development engineer would form a team with production and marketing people to develop, produce, and market a new product.

- Respect and loyalty—Bill Hewlett and Dave Packard believed that by being loyal to employees and treating them with respect, the employees would be loyal to them, and in this way they would create a culture of trust. When there was a downturn in business everyone, including Hewlett and Packard, took a twenty percent cut in salary and a day off, rather than laying anyone off. The value of respect was put to the test when HP initiated a division to produce computers. The people they hired to lead the division didn't share the HP values; they were disrespectful and uncooperative. Hewlett fired them and started again with people who practiced what he called the "HP Way."

- Entrepreneurial behavior—HP thrived on innovative products and processes. Hewlett wanted to hire entrepreneurs. I questioned whether entrepreneurs would leave HP to start their own companies. Yes, Hewlett said, but he believed that, treated well, these entrepreneurs would become good suppliers and customers to HP.

And that's what happened. Entrepreneurs left HP and built companies, like Steve Wozniak who, with Steven Jobs, started Apple. HP's philosophy not only built HP, it also contributed to the Silicon Valley miracle.

An organizational philosophy based on the leadership philosophy of founders has to be continually affirmed by the leaders that follow them. HP's philosophy did not last. As HP grew, acquired companies with different values, and hired outsiders as CEOs, the HP Way was lost. Current employees have told me and my colleagues that the company has suffered a loss of purpose and trust.

Maintaining a Philosophy

When I began to work as a consultant and coach to AT&T management in 1978, the company was a national monopoly. Although it was a bureaucracy with uniform roles and processes, personal relationships could cut through the red tape. There was an implicit organizational philosophy that reflected the leadership philosophy expressed by Theodore Vail at the start of the twentieth century. The purpose of AT&T was universal telephone service, and the supporting values included service for all customers, regardless of their income or status; respect for employees; being good citizens in all communities served; and technological excellence. AT&T was especially proud of the Bell Labs, its Nobel Prize-winning R&D arm that equipped the operating divisions of the Bell System with new technology.

After the breakup of the Bell System in 1984, I continued to work with AT&T and its unions until 2000. But the implicit philosophy was no longer relevant, and the slogans put in its place inspired no one. AT&T had become a competitive business. The trust engendered by the paternalistic promise of lifetime employment had dissolved in huge lay-offs. All customers no longer merited the same gold-plated service. You got what you paid for. Well-meaning leaders struggled to make the company competitive, but they seemed unaware of the need for an inspiring philosophy. Managers looked out for themselves more than for each other or for customers.

In contrast to HP and AT&T, the philosophy William Mayo used to build Mayo Clinic has been continually affirmed and developed by Mayo Clinic staff. It has helped to create and sustain one of the best healthcare organizations in the world and has facilitated effective organizational change.[1]

William Mayo's thinking and actions demonstrated strategic intelligence. He had the foresight to scan for innovations in medicine and to seek new opportunities. He envisioned an innovative collaborative organization. He partnered with others who shared his philosophy, and he engaged and inspired collaborators with his vision, supported by a powerful philosophy.

Mayo described his clinic's purpose in terms of a primary value: *the needs of the patient come first.* A major supporting value was collaborative medicine for the benefit of the patient. Unlike most healthcare organizations, where patients with complex problems have to make appointments with specialists in different departments, at Mayo Clinic patients are met and cared for by a physician who makes the appointments and manages collaboration among all the patient's care providers. In most medical organizations, doctors don't criticize each other. At Mayo, the culture supports criticism based on patient wellbeing.

From the start, Mayo partnered with the Sisters of St Francis, who ran a hospital nearby in Rochester, Minnesota. When I interviewed some of the sisters in 2001, they praised Mayo Clinic physicians for their cooperation and respectful relations with the nurses. In most academic health organizations I've studied or consulted to, nurses complain of lack of respect. Doctors don't listen to their views about patients. Mayo Clinic physicians treat nurses as partners. The hospital administrator summarized the relationship, "We accept doctors as leaders, but not as bosses."

William Mayo also valued continual research. He went anywhere in the world where surgeons were practicing a new technique, stayed long enough to learn it, and on his return, taught it to Mayo Clinic surgeons. In 2012, Mayo Clinic invested $633.5 million in research. All physicians are encouraged to participate in clinical research, and clinical findings are shared with six other leading healthcare organizations.

From its start, 150 years ago, Mayo Clinic has grown from a single clinic in Rochester, Minnesota to campuses in 73 communities, a medical school, and research facilities, all united by William Mayo's philosophy, continually re-affirmed by Mayo Clinic leadership.

In its 2012 annual report, Mayo Clinic's mission or purpose is stated as:

> To inspire hope and contribute to health and well-being by providing the best care to every patient through integrated clinical practice, education and research.

To support this purpose, Mayo Clinic staff commit to "live our values of collaboration, compassion and innovation."

An organization's philosophy is not complete without describing a method of evaluating or measuring results that supports the purpose and values. Most organizations publish lists of values, but in many cases, the measurements do not support the values, and may even contradict them. According to studies of global companies in different countries led by Berth Jönsson at Stockholm-based TNS SIFO, 70 percent of employees say their company has values that have been communicated to them. Sixty-five percent can name these values, but only 47 percent of the 65 percent say that they believe in and act on these values. This is only 31 percent of those who participated in the study, leaving

69 percent who do not believe in and act in terms of the espoused values.[2] An organizational value is meaningful when it is practiced and reinforced by measurements.

Mayo Clinic not only measures results in terms of financials and the number of patients treated in its network. Every week patients are randomly surveyed about their treatment experience to gain information to improve the service. Quality of patient care is also measured in terms of mortality rates, surgical infections, safety, readmission rates, and compliance with evidence-based processes known to enhance care. Employee attitudes are also measured. When I surveyed Mayo Clinic physicians and administrators, I found a high level of satisfaction and trust, based on affirmations that the values were being practiced.

Mayo Clinic also values operating efficiently and minimizing its impact on the environment by the use of renewable energy such as solar panels, recycling, and adding low-flow aerators to reduce water consumption. In 2012, Mayo Clinic leaders worked across sites to develop a scorecard to benchmark, streamline, and continuously improve performance in energy usage, waste management, and supply chain practices.

Mayo Clinic's mission of hope extends to extensive charity care and help for victims of floods in the US and the earthquake in Haiti. I am an advisor to leaders at Nuestros Pequeños Hermanos (NPH), a charitable organization that has benefitted from Mayo Clinic's humanitarian outreach.

Nuestros Pequeños Hermanos—NPH (Our Little Brothers and Sisters)

Mayo Clinic physicians came to help after the earthquake in 2010 and continue to volunteer their services to the St Damien Pediatric Hospital in Tabarre, Haiti, a part of NPH or *Nos Petits Fréres et Soeurs* (NPFS), a home for orphaned and abandoned children founded in Mexico in 1954 by William Wasson, an American priest. Father Wasson came to Mexico to teach adolescent psychology at Mexico City College. A bishop in Arizona had refused to ordain him because of his chronic thyroid condition, but he was ordained by the bishop of Cuernavaca, who placed him in a small church near the marketplace. One day, the poor box was robbed and the thief, a little boy was caught and sent to jail by the sacristan. Wasson went to the jail and asked the warden to release the boy, but the warden said he was homeless and would be soon back in jail. Wasson offered to make a home for him. The warden handed over the boy and soon after, brought Wasson more homeless orphans. So began NPH.

To shorten a story of 60 years, NPH now has homes in Mexico, Guatemala, El Salvador, Honduras, Nicaragua, Peru, Bolivia, Haiti, and Dominican Republic.

In 2013, over 3,500 children were cared for in these homes, and thousands more benefitted from NPH's schools, clinics, and the pediatric hospital. Founded and directed by Father Richard Frechette, a priest and physician who came to NPH as a young volunteer, St Damien's treated over 90,000 children during 2013.

The directors of five of the nine homes grew up at NPH, as did Miguel Venegas, the executive director of NPH International. All have university degrees. The other four homes are led by former volunteers from Europe and the US.

When NPH began to grow, Wasson studied orphanages in the US. He was impressed by the facilities at Boys Town in Omaha, Nebraska, but he felt it was an institution rather than a home. He especially disliked the rule that the boys had to leave the orphanage at the age of 18. Wasson wanted to build a family, not an institution, where brothers and sisters cared for each other and the children could stay until they felt ready to live independently. He decided to accept all the children in a family and not to allow adoption, because it would separate siblings and also favor cuter kids.

In 1973, he described to me his organizational philosophy.

Father William Wasson's Philosophy for Nuestros Pequeños Hermanos

The purpose of NPH is not only to provide a caring home for orphaned and abandoned children, but to develop them as good Christians who care about others in need and who also are equipped to be productive citizens and leaders in their own countries.

The values essential to achieve this purpose are as follows:

1. *Basic security*—the children should feel they never have to leave. They should feel loved and cared for. Excellent schooling is also a part of security. A good education prepares children for employment and gives them a sense of security. (NPH supports the schooling of children as far as they are able to go. Some have become doctors, lawyers, teachers, engineers, etc. Others are trained in NPH workshops to be electricians, carpenters, dress makers, etc.)

2. *Work*—children should feel they are earning their own way. Work balances basic security so that children don't become passive. Even small children should have tasks. This also includes a year of service to a home after graduation from high school.

3. *Sharing*—the children should be brought up to care about others. They should visit hospitals and prisons. This is a way of combating

egocentrism and selfishness. It is also a way of avoiding *pobre de me*, "poor-little-me" self-pity that weakens a person and reinforces egocentrism. Prayer should focus on developing kindness.

4. *Responsibility and co-responsibility*—responsibility is the ability to respond ethically and morally, as in contrast with following rules. Children learn the reasons why they should act responsibly individually and together with others.

This philosophy has sustained NPH as a family, not an institution. Father Wasson saw himself as the father of the children, and he expected older children to be caring older brothers and sisters to the younger children. In his sermons, he preached his philosophy and the importance of love defined as agápe, caring, and commitment based on knowledge of another person combined with a generous heart.[3] I have met periodically with NPH leaders to affirm the philosophy, discuss how it is being practiced, and what needs to be done to improve practices.

Organizational Philosophy and Human Development

NPH shows that when a powerful philosophy is practiced, an organization can stimulate human development. Children coming from extreme poverty, and in many cases violence that destroyed their families, are raised to be productive, hopeful, caring, and collaborative.

What about collaborative organizations that hire grown-up people? Do they sustain collaboration by selecting collaborative people? Or can a strong collaborative philosophy create a culture that develops collaborative behavior? Mayo Clinic favors hiring doctors who have graduated from its medical school and have been practicing collaboration. However, IBM professionals tell me that the company culture became much more collaborative when Sam Palmisano became CEO and engaged managers world-wide in developing values and incentives to support collaboration. In both cases, a collaborative and humanly developing culture has been sustained when leaders communicated, practiced, and engaged others in implementing a supportive philosophy.

The philosophies and actions of leaders can move the culture of organizations (even countries) and the social character of people either in the direction of human development or in the negative direction of conformity and tribalism. In *The Heart of Man*,[4] Erich Fromm described human development, consistent with all the great humanistic religious, as individuation, love of the stranger, and *biophilia* (love of life). By individuation, Fromm meant something similar to Father Wasson's value of responsibility, doing the right thing, not out of fear of punishment, but in response to a humanistic conscience, a heart that listens. This is different from individualism, which can be self-centered.

Fromm proposed the term "biophilia" to describe attraction to and protection of life and support of harmony, freedom, and creative growth, as contrasted to rigid control, exploitation, and destructiveness. The concept is similar to what Albert Schweitzer, the missionary physician and theologian, termed *reverence for life*.[5]

No culture can develop these qualities in everyone, but it can support growth in this direction as opposed to the direction of conformity, tribalism, and exploitation. Fromm drew a figure contrasting elements of human development, the syndrome of growth, in contrast to human pathology, the syndrome of decay (see Figure 4.2). I have added the elements that contrast collaborative learning communities with tribalistic organizations.

A productive leadership philosophy and organizational culture can support a collaborative community, a learning organization that respects individuals and the environment. Organizations that move in this direction are the most innovative. A bureaucracy typically falls somewhere in the middle of the diamond, while a tribal organization demands conformity, total identification with the organization, exploitation of the environment, and hostility to outsiders. Tribalism was the social character that Hitler and Stalin tried to shape by force, moving their societies toward autocratic group-think and group narcissism that rationalized exploitation and destructiveness by defining other groups as less than human.

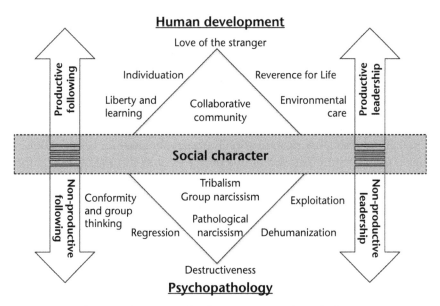

Figure 4.2. Human development vs psychopathology

In contrast, the framers of the Constitution of the United States designed an organizational philosophy meant to develop a society that both furthers the common good and protects individual liberty. The purpose of the Constitution is stated in its preamble.

We the People of the United States, in Order to form a more perfect Union, establish Justice, insure domestic Tranquility, provide for the common defense, promote the general Welfare, and secure the Blessings of Liberty to ourselves and our Posterity, do ordain and establish this Constitution of the United States of America.

This purpose is supported by a democratic legislature and the values expressed in the first ten amendments that protect free speech, religion, and due process. The Constitution combines a purpose that requires collaboration and rights that protect individuals from abusive government power. And it includes processes for changing the Constitution to better serve its purpose.

Over two centuries, Americans have debated the meaning of the purpose and values stated in the Constitution. They have added amendments, including these that expand the meaning and protection of liberty:

- the first 10 amendments and the Bill of Rights, to clarify the purpose of establishing justice and securing the blessings of liberty;
- the 14th amendment, and the civil rights legislation of the 1950s and 1960s to expand these rights to African-Americans;
- the 19th amendment to grant women's voting rights.

The framers had been thinking systemically about the Constitution as they prepared for the convention that drafted it.

James Madison, in *The Federalist*, Numbers 10 and 50, emphasized that a system of checks and balances—what eventually became the executive, legislative, and judicial branches—would be necessary to protect individual liberty. Without this system, democracy could lead to oppression of individuals and minorities by majority factions.

On a grand scale, American history illustrates the need for organizations to develop a philosophy and supportive processes, and continually both affirm and revise that philosophy to better achieve the organization's purpose.

How to Develop a Leadership Philosophy for an Organization

An organizational philosophy is a key element in an effective social system. It answers four interrelated questions:

1. What is the *purpose* of our organization?
2. What *practical values* do we need to practice to further our purpose?

3. What *ethical* and *moral* reasoning determines the key decisions we make?

4. How do we define and measure *results* so that they support our purpose and values?

THE MEANING OF PURPOSE

Purpose describes the reason for the organization, its *raison d'etre*. Many organizations use the term *mission* to describe their organization's purpose. The *OED* defines mission as "the act of sending someone to perform some function or service" or "an important assignment carried out for political, religious, or commercial purposes." In terms of this definition, missions are limited in time. In contrast, the *OED* defines purpose as "the reason for which something is done or created or for which something exists."

A purpose can require flexibility, changes in products and services to adapt to changing markets. Bill Hewlett's purpose of making tools that helped technicians to perform better led him to add computers to the product mix. If the buggy-whip producers of the nineteenth century had defined their purpose as vehicle acceleration, rather than buggy-whip manufacture, they might still be in business, manufacturing parts for different types of vehicles.

W. Edwards Deming equated purpose with a company's definition of its business. In a conversation I had with him in 1992, he said:

> Where today are the makers of carburetors? They're gone. Twenty-five years ago, every automobile had at least one carburetor. How could it run without one? And within the space of a year, the makers of carburetors were out of the picture. They made better and better carburetors, at lower and lower cost. They had happy customers. What more could anybody ask for? They went out of business because they were in the business of making carburetors. They should have seen them-selves in the business to put a stoichiometric mixture of fuel and air into the combustion chamber and the best way to do it. It came with the fuel injector. It does that job and a lot more. One must think about the future, prepare for it and make your own future, not be a victim.

Many companies define their purpose as profit or return to shareholders. But no one except shareholders is inspired by this purpose and it does not focus a company on its future. John Mackay of Whole Foods writes that profits are a means to the end of fulfilling Whole Foods' business mission or purpose, "to improve the health and well-being of everyone on the planet through higher-quality foods and better nutrition."[6] That is a purpose that can inspire employees and customers.

After citing Mackay, Bill George, former CEO of Medtronic, writes that "busi-ness should start with its purpose and values and use them to inspire employees to innovate and provide superior service, while creating sustainable increases in revenues and profits." He goes on to write that this philosophy is "practiced at such diverse firms as IBM, Starbucks, Apple, Novartis, Wells Fargo and General Mills, all of which have sustained great success for decades."[7]

Soichiro Honda, the founder of the automobile and motorcycle company, stated that his purpose was to satisfy a social need. He viewed the development of the low-pollution CVCC engine as an answer to air contamination and pollution problems. The R&D technicians who developed the engine were inspired not by the promise of profit, but by the challenge of improving the environment.[8]

To succeed, a company has to attract and maintain customers and talented employees. In recently held leadership workshops I have led, those led by Tim Scudder, and those we've done together, leaders from companies and government agencies have recognized the value of developing an organizational philosophy that attracts customers and inspires employees.

They start by defining purpose. This may take a number of sessions. With one company, we began the process with the top thirty executives. In groups of six, they proposed statements of purpose. These were collected and written on flip charts. The group then voted and one was overwhelmingly selected. The statement of purpose, together with supporting values, was considered in workshops with the next level of management. Suggested edits were returned to the CEO who, together with colleagues, produced a final draft which was approved by the board.

Once there is a statement of organizational purpose, support groups such as finance and HR should define their purpose of strengthening the organization. Usually, the first attempts at purpose statements are too long; a good purpose statement is short and inspiring.

PRACTICAL VALUES

Purpose will inspire employees and customers only when it is backed up by practical values, the beliefs and behaviors that have to be practiced in order to achieve the organization's purpose. I have described the practical values that support the purposes of HP, Mayo Clinic, and NPH.

Practical values may be called by other names—guiding principles, shared values, targeted behaviors, etc. Whatever they are called, they need to be practiced throughout the organization to achieve its purpose and implement its vision.

If an organization changes its purpose, it will probably have to change some of the practical values that support it. For example, companies I've worked with have changed their purpose from producing excellent products to helping customers succeed with their products and services. Typically, a purely product-focused purpose is supported by values that emphasize excellence of design, engineering, and continuous improvement of product and processes. When the purpose is helping a customer succeed, supportive practical values typically include collaboration, within the company and with customers, understanding the customer's business, and innovation.

PRINCIPLED PRAGMATISM

When Abraham Lincoln became President of the United States, he took an oath to protect the Constitution and maintain the union. Lincoln believed the right of liberty should extend to slaves, and while running for office, he had condemned slavery as evil. However, at the start of the Civil War, when General John C. Fremont proclaimed the slaves in Missouri liberated, Lincoln fired him and reversed the proclamation. He reasoned that he had no legal right to end slavery and that by freeing the slaves at the start of the war, he would lose the slave-holding Border States; the South would win the war and spread slavery to the West. Later in the war, when he was able to show that the South was using slaves to strengthen its armies, Lincoln was able to argue that freeing the slaves would weaken the enemy. He then issued the Emancipation Proclamation as a practical as well as a moral decision. Before the end of the war, he worked to persuade Congress to pass the 14th amendment to the Constitution that made slavery illegal.

Sometimes values will clash. There may not be time to gain collaboration to address an urgent problem. A doctor at Mayo Clinic might have to act quickly to save the life of a patient. A child at NPH may act destructively. To protect his security would jeopardize the security of other children. While professing and practicing organizational values, leaders may have to be *principled pragmatists* who interpret these values to support the organization's purpose.

ETHICAL AND MORAL REASONING

How we make decisions depends on our philosophy, what we value. This includes our ethical and moral reasoning. I have found it useful to view ethics not only as rules set by religion, law, and professional rules of conduct, but also as the values that underlie these rules. These include values essential to building trust, such as honesty, respect, and doing no harm. Ethical behavior not only builds trust, it keeps people out of serious trouble with the law and regulatory agencies. Ethical behavior should be expected of everyone in an organization. However, the application of ethics depends on the level of moral reasoning practiced in an organization.

LEVELS OF MORAL REASONING

Laurence Kohlberg[9] studied levels of moral reasoning in terms of a person's definition of "the good" and described the following three levels:

1. The lowest level defines the good as individual wellbeing, gained by avoiding punishment and getting what you want. This implies that a

person conforms to ethical rules only when an authority is watching or might subsequently learn about an infraction. With this kind of morality, there is no common good. It's only looking out for number one.

2. The next level defines the good in terms of what people consider good for their families or organizations as well as for themselves, without concern for the effect of their actions on those outside their circle. This definition can lead to a narrow view of the common good: we versus others. It can strengthen a tribalistic organization. Or it can be a start of viewing self-interest in terms of the larger community that supports the organization.

3. A broader definition of the common good is what benefits, or at least doesn't harm, all those who may be affected by one's actions. This might include employees, customers, owners, communities, unborn generations, and the natural environment. This definition supports the organization as a collaborative community.

At this third level of moral reasoning, leaders may be challenged to make tough decisions that don't benefit themselves or their organizations, but will benefit the larger common good. A decision like this requires moral courage. However, a decision that does not benefit an organization in the short term may do so for the longer term. A notable example was the 1982 decision by Johnson & Johnson's CEO to withdraw and destroy all Tylenol in stores because some capsules had been poisoned. This costly decision created public trust in the company and its products.

Robert Wood Johnson crafted a company philosophy in 1943 that began "We believe our first responsibility is to the doctors, nurses and patients . . . who use our products." However, the company did not live up to this promise or the Tylenol example, when it waited nearly two years after receiving a warning from doctors before withdrawing a faulty hip implant from the market.[10]

The level of moral reasoning at which a leader and an organization operate can be inferred by the way that purpose, practical values, and definition of results are expressed. Examples of company intentions to practice a high level of moral reasoning include:

- *Google*—Sergey Brin and Larry Page, founders of Google, express the philosophy of "Do no harm." Their document "Ten Things We Know to Be True"[11] invites people to hold the organization accountable for acting in accordance with the ten things, including "You can make money without doing evil."

- *General Electric*—General Electric's slogan "We bring good things to life" has been used not just in marketing, but also to focus employees on the meaning of "good things" from the view of their customers, communities, and more recently, the environment.

• Whole Foods—leadership has stated moral aspirations including:

We want to help evolve the world's agricultural system to be both efficient and sustainable. This includes a much higher level of livestock animal welfare, seafood sustainability, and upgraded efficiency and productivity of organic agriculture.

We want to raise the public's collective awareness about the principles of healthy eating: a diet that is centered on whole foods is primarily plant based, is nutrient dense, and includes mainly healthy fats (minimal animal fats and vegetable oils). We believe that diet will radically improve the health of millions of people by helping prevent and reverse the lifestyle diseases that are killing so many of us—heart disease, stroke, cancer, diabetes, and obesity.[12]

By articulating a philosophy that includes a higher level of moral reasoning, leaders strengthen the focus on customer and community and inspire collaborators to think of the wellbeing not only of themselves and the organization, but also of the community and environment that supports the organization.

When I interviewed corporate leaders in the 1970s, a common attitude to corporate social responsibility, or what is now termed *sustainability* was that the business of business was to be profitable. Even though a CEO might privately be an environmentalist, protection of the environment was not his job. It was the job of government. One CEO told me, "I like the game to be defined. Our main ability is that we know how to win at the game of business. Society can make any rules it wants, as long as they are clear-cut, the same for everyone. We can win at any game society can invent."[13]

Recently, in workshops with business executives, I have asked them to indicate the level of moral decision making they practice or want to practice. Over time, I've found more leaders aspiring to reach level three. As an exercise, I have asked these leaders to consider an ethical or moral issue they face and how they should address it.

The CEO of a large European department store reported that he was concerned about selling products made by children in Pakistani factories, but he had been told that if the children did not have this work, they would lack money for food. He proposed as a level-three moral decision having the children work half a day and attend a school in the factory the other half-day. This is a creative solution to a moral challenge, but he found that it was not easy to implement and when I wrote this, he was still working on it.

DEFINITION OF RESULTS
Values are strengthened when they are supported by the organization's measurements. All businesses include measures of financial results in their annual

reports. Some, but not all, of the companies that proclaim idealistic or level-three values publish supporting measures.

- The 2013 GE annual report states, "We are committed to finding sustainable solutions to benefit the planet, its people and the economy." GE employs the GRI (Global Reporting Initiative) Sustainability Reporting Guidelines and reports measures of the company's impact on the environment, labor practices, human rights, product responsibility, and communities.

- The John Lewis Partnership, the third largest UK private company, publishes a sustainability report, with measures similar to those reported by GE. The importance of the value of collaboration is demonstrated both among employee-owners and in partnering with suppliers, especially farmers, to the company's retail stores.

- Although Whole Foods has an even more ambitious purpose and espoused values than the John Lewis Partnership, the annual report includes fewer measures that support purpose and values. The company does report loans to local farmers and partnering with other organizations to put healthy salad bars in US and Canadian schools. But there are no measures reported as evidence for the statement, "We support team member happiness and excellence."

- United Airlines, one of the early innovators in flight safety and Crew Resource Management (CRM) training, reports passenger safety measures as a higher priority than on-time arrivals and profitability.

- The US National Park Service describes results that support the purpose that was legislated by Congress, " ... to promote and regulate the use of the ... national parks ... which purpose is to conserve the scenery and the natural and historic objects and the wild life therein and to provide for the enjoyment of the same in such manner and by such means as will leave them unimpaired for the enjoyment of future generations." Results are defined and measured in service, environmental restoration, and effective partnering, which includes sharing technical information and expertise with other organizations. Tim Scudder and I led a series of leadership workshops with the US National Park Service managers, who expressed enthusiasm for working to achieve the organization's purpose.

Even from a practical point of view, it makes sense for businesses to keep track of more than the bottom line, for this is a trailing indicator, describing past results. Future success depends on factors like hiring, retaining, and developing talent and finding and satisfying customer needs. By measuring these leading indicators, companies keep track of the qualities essential for sustainable success.

A Tool for Maintaining an Organizational Philosophy

Communicating an organizational philosophy is not enough to maintain it. Leaders should also initiate a dialogue with all parts of the organization about the values, their importance for achieving the organization's purpose, and the degree to which they are being practiced. A useful tool to facilitate such a dialogue is a gap survey. People in different parts of an organization may have different views of the importance of the practical values to achieving the organization's purpose, and they may also have different views about how well they are being practiced (see Table 4.1).

A gap survey for a company that aspires to be a learning organization with the purpose of helping customers to succeed might use surveys of value gaps like this with different groups.

When there are gaps of two places or more, leaders should initiate a discussion about the meaning of the gap and what it would take to close the gap.

When importance is higher than practice, a leader should ask for examples and suggestions of actions that would close the gap. There may be differences in how people rate importance and practice. A leader should facilitate discussion about these differences that may be caused by different experiences (see Table 4.2). Once everyone has had a say, it is up to a leader to decide what needs to be done and to assign tasks to close the gaps. This may demand systemic changes in processes.

When practice is scored higher than importance, the practiced value may be seen as more important in different parts of the organization, or there may be differences in views about priorities.

Table 4.1. Example of a survey of value gaps

	How important is this value for achieving the organization's purpose?		How well are we practicing this values?	
	Not important	Very important	Not well	Very well
• Collaboration	1 2 3	4 5	1 2 3	4 5
• Participation in continuous improvement	1 2 3	4 5	1 2 3	4 5
• Shared learning	1 2 3	4 5	1 2 3	4 5
• Innovation	1 2 3	4 5	1 2 3	4 5

Table 4.2. Closing value gaps

Value gap	Evidence to support gaps	Action(s) required
1		
2		

When I was consulting to an academic healthcare organization, the university vice president leading the organization put "service to the community" as one of the values on a gap survey given to the department chairs. Some chairs gave it a 4 and others gave it a 2 in importance. Asked why the value was scored so low, one chair argued that the organization was losing money and could not afford charitable community service. Asked why the value was scored 4, another chair argued that the organization was exempted from taxes and benefitted from a number of city services such as transportation, policing, etc. and that to maintain their benefits, it made sense to give something back to the city. The vice-president agreed.

Although they had been overruled, the chairs who had scored the value 2 were satisfied that they had been heard and that the decision was reasonable. Without a gap survey and facilitated dialogue, a discussion about the importance of community service might have been dominated by one or two of the most vocal chairs. Those who disagreed with them might have kept silent to avoid conflict.

Gap surveys may produce different results in different parts of an organization. Operations focused on external customers have different ways of practicing an organization's values than do the finance department and human resource department focused on internal customers.

When values are aligned with practice on the survey, leaders should ask collaborators for evidence of this and thoughts about either maintaining a high-rated value or revising or eliminating one rated low on both importance and practice (see Table 4.3).

Leadership and Organizational Philosophies

The organizational philosophies of Mayo Clinic, HP, and NPH expressed the leadership philosophies of William Mayo, Bill Hewlett and Dave Packard, and William Wasson. Because their leadership philosophies were consistent with their personal philosophies, they were seen as authentic; they were trusted and followed. This has been the case with other founders of great companies. Henry Ford's purpose was to produce a car most people could afford. Steve Jobs' purpose was to produce beautiful products that empowered people. These purposes and the supporting organizational values were not public relations slogans but deeply held life purposes. Leaders will be most effective when their personal philosophy is consistent with their leadership philosophy and the philosophy of the organization they lead. As discussed in Chapter 6, we all have philosophies, including our purpose in life, the values we practice to achieve that purpose, how we make ethical and moral decisions, and how we evaluate the results of our actions.

Figure 4.3. Personal, leadership, and organizational philosophies

A leadership philosophy will be different from a personal philosophy but only if they are consistent will it be experienced as authentic and inspiring (see Figure 4.3).

Table 4.3. Practice aligned with value

Aligned value	Evidence to support the alignment rating	Action(s) required
1		
2		

Questions About Your Leadership Philosophy

1. What is your purpose as a leader?
2. What is the purpose of the organization you lead? What should it be?
3. How does your purpose as a leader reflect your personal philosophy?
4. How does your purpose as a leader support the purpose of your organization?
5. At what level of moral reasoning do you want to operate?
6. What are the practical values that need to be practiced to support your leadership purpose?
7. How do you define results so they are consistent with your purpose and values?

Notes

1. In 2012, the Mayo Clinic Model of Care prompted a number of organizations that rank US hospitals on patient safety, outcomes, and satisfaction to again name Mayo Clinic as one of the best in the country.

   Leapfrog is a highly regarded independent organization that compares safety, quality, and efficiency at hospitals across the country. It named Mayo Clinic a Top

Hospital. The University HealthSystem Consortium awarded it a Quality Leadership Award, making Mayo one of only ten institutions to receive the award.

U.S. News & World Report ranked Mayo Clinic No. 1 in the nation in diabetes and endocrinology, gastroenterology, and gynecology. It also ranked Mayo in the top four in ten other specialties: cancer, neurology and neurosurgery, orthopedics, pulmonology, rheumatology, nephrology, urology, and cardiology and heart surgery.

2. Personal communication from Berth Jönsson.
3. Agápe is defined in Matthew 22: 37–40 and Paul, Corinthians, 1: 13.
4. Erich Fromm, *The Heart of Man* (New York: Harper Row, 1964).
5. Albert Schweitzer, 'The Ethics of Reverence for Life', *Christendom* (1936) 1: 225–39.
6. John Mackey and Rajendra Sisodia, *Conscious Capitalism: Liberating the Heroic Spirit of Business* (Boston, MA: Harvard Business School Press, 2013), p. xii.
7. John Mackey and Rajendra Sisodia, *Conscious Capitalism: Liberating the Heroic Spirit of Business* (Boston, MA: Harvard Business School Press, 2013), p. xii.
8. Sol W. Sanders, *Honda: The Man and His Machines* (Boston, MA: Little Brown & Co., 1975), p. 38.
9. Laurence Kohlberg, "The Claim to Moral Adequacy of a Highest Stage of Moral Judgment," *The Journal of Philosophy* 70(18) (1973): 630–46.
10. Barry Meier, "Doctors Who Don't Speak Out," *New York Times* (15 February 2013).
11. Google, "Ten Things We Know to Be True," at: <http://www.google.com/about/company/philosophy/> (accessed November 2014).
12. John Mackey and R. Sisodia, *Conscious Capitalism: Liberating the Heroic Spirit of Business* (Boston, MA: Harvard Business School Press, 2013), p. 64.
13. Michael Maccoby, *The Gamesman* (New York: Simon & Schuster, 1976), p. 120.

5

Visioning Change

*Humans are more than ends-seeking animals; we are **ideal-seeking**. Curiously, however, this characteristic of humans is ignored in all approaches to planning other than the interactive.*

—Russell L. Ackoff

In one sense, involvement in planning is like playing a game that one wants to win, but the winning of which is not the principal benefit to be obtained from the play...Planning should be fun as well as productive. If it is, it enhances the quality of work life of the participants and enables them to be developed.

—Russell L. Ackoff, *Creating the Corporate Future*

A leader or leadership team with strategic intelligence may judge that threats and opportunities call for change. To maintain constancy of purpose, they may need to change the organization. They may even need to change both purpose and organization to stay in business.

Transformation from a bureaucracy to a learning organization engages all the elements of strategic intelligence. An essential element is visioning (see Figure 5.1). Russell Ackoff did not use the term "vision," but his concepts of idealized design and interactive planning are essential tools for developing a vision of organizational transformation.

This chapter describes Ackoff's concepts and how I applied and built on them.

I got to know Russ at Volvo where he was a consultant to Bo Ekman, the vice president of strategy and I was working with Berth Jönsson, the vice president of human resources and other Volvo managers on improving productivity. I learned about visioning as idealized design both from Ackoff's writings and directly from him when he brought me into his work with Canadian Pacific.

In 1994, before we began to work together, Ackoff and I were recorded discussing our experiences of changing organizations.[1] I described how I had helped executives to lead change. Ackoff described how different change agents, in this case Russ and I, approach their work differently. He said,

> It seems to me that there's a very interesting difference in the way we approach the same problem in the same context. Coming from psychology, as you do, what you

Figure 5.1 Strategic intelligence: focus on visioning

try to do is change the individual in such a way that he will operate on his environment differently than he did before you came along. I don't have that set of skills, and therefore my approach is how do I change the environment so that it will change his behavior? You're coming at the environment through the person, I'm coming at the person through the environment. So I try to change the way he's organized, how he interacts with other people rather than his perception of himself or the problem, saying that that will come as a result of the changes in the way he has to operate. You're saying, I'm going to change the way he operates by changing his perception of what's going on. I think we're complementary.

Ackoff added, "We're not saying there is a handbook that everybody can use. The transformation of an organization basically uses science, but there is no set of rules you can follow mechanically and expect to produce the corporation of tomorrow. It's a work of art." I agreed with Russ, and I enjoyed working with and learning from him.

Ackoff's Concept of Corporate Transformation

In his masterwork, *Creating the Corporate Future*,[2] Ackoff viewed the process of corporate transformation in an historical context. It helps to follow his thinking to fully appreciate the conceptual tools he designed. At the start of the

Industrial Revolution, corporations were viewed as "machines whose function was to serve their owner-creators with an adequate return on their investment of time and money."[3] Employees were treated as parts of the machine, and as such had no rights.

> In the early part of the 20th century, this concept began to change. Corporations went public with dispersed ownership. More educated workers were needed. Unionization and the threat of unionization forced managers to improve working conditions. After World War 1 a new concept of the corporation gradually emerged: the corporation as an *organism*. So conceptualized, the corporation was taken to have a life and purpose of its own. Its principal purpose, like those of any organism, were believed to be **survival** and **growth**. Corporate profit came to be viewed in much the same way as oxygen is to an organism—necessary, but not the reason for its existence.[4]

In this concept, management became the brain and workers were like organs that responded to the brain's commands. But as work became more complex and workers acquired more skills, the command-and-control approach to management no longer worked well. Employees needed some autonomy to solve problems and innovate. Furthermore, they were turned off by work that did not engage their head as well as their hands.

Ackoff was writing at the very start of the age of knowledge work. He had the foresight to see the emergence of a new concept of the corporation as a *social system*, a purposeful system, parts of which—people—have purposes of their own. This system had to be able to innovate and adapt to a constantly changing environment. To do so, leaders needed conceptual tools based on science, and the art to employ them.

Ackoff's Science and Art

Ackoff's science and conceptual tools include the following, which I have found extremely useful for leading change:

- systems thinking;
- idealized design;
- interactive planning.

I will describe each one of these conceptual tools and how I've used it.

Systems Thinking

As noted in Chapter 2, systems thinking is essential for designing and implementing a vision. Without it, a vision is unlikely to be effective. However, for the executives my colleagues and I have interviewed and taught, systems thinking is the biggest gap in their strategic intelligence. Their knee-jerk approach to a problem is to attack and analyze, to break it into manageable pieces that are stacked rather than integrated.

Bureaucracies are built with analytic thinking. Individual roles are designed to perform a function. Groups of these roles are then coordinated and controlled by the next higher level and so on, building a hierarchy like a Lego construction. In contrast, systems thinking for a learning organization starts with defining the organization's purpose within a larger system or context that includes customers, suppliers, regulators, etc. The organization is then designed holistically to achieve its purpose.

Ackoff proposes three criteria that define a system of two or more elements.

1. The behavior of each element has an effect on the behavior of the whole.
2. No element has an independent effect on the system as a whole. The elements are interdependent.
3. Subgroups of the system are not independent, as they might be in a bureaucracy.

It follows that a system is a whole that cannot be divided into independent parts, and every system has properties that none of its parts have by themselves. (For example, no part of a human body can run. No part of a car can drive down a road.) Ackoff concludes that "The essential properties of a system taken as a whole are derived from the *interactions* of the parts, not their actions taken separately. Therefore, *when a system is taken apart it loses its essential properties. Because of this—and this is the critical point—a system is a whole that cannot be understood by analysis.*"[5]

Systems thinking starts with three steps, which are the opposite of traditional analytical thinking (see Table 5.1). In analytical thought, we take things apart to understand the parts and then aggregate them to explain the whole. Systems thinking requires that we first consider the larger whole, in which the element we want to understand is a part. Then we describe the elements in terms of their role or function within the system.

Table 5.1. Analytic and systems thinking

	Analytic thinking	Systems thinking
1	Take something apart or break it into components or sub-processes	Identify the system or context in which the element to be explained is a part
2	Explain the properties and behaviors of each of the parts	Explain the behavior or properties of the system
3	Aggregate the understanding of the parts to understand and explain the whole	Then explain the behavior or properties of each element in terms of its role(s) or function(s) within the system

To improve the effectiveness of an organization, analytic thinking would lead to separating the components of the organization and studying each one with the intent to improve each component in order to improve the function of the total organization. Systems thinking would cause us to first consider the larger system or context in which the organization operates (e.g. the financial system, the transportation system, the communication system, the energy system, the education system, the government system, the national defense system). After we explain the behavior of the bigger system or context, we can begin to understand and explain the role the organization plays within it. After the role of the organization has been explained at this level, we can begin to consider the parts of the organization. We can ask "How does the part of the organization (e.g. marketing, manufacturing, human resources) interact and function with the other parts of the organization to achieve its purpose?"

In designing an organizational vision, we should use both analytic thinking and systems thinking. We need to start with understanding the organization's purpose, then design the elements, analyze how they will interact, and then plan the implementation.

Idealized Design—the Leader as Architect

Ackoff's concept of an organizational vision was rooted in his training as an architect. In our discussion, he said that the customer should be allowed to design the product or service they want, but he went on to describe an example of what he meant in terms of an architect's process in designing a house.

> For example, when a family comes to an architect saying, "We want to build a house. We'd like it to be modern architecture, three bedrooms, a playroom," and so on, and they give all the specifications, and the architect produces a drawing. That's not the end, that's only the beginning because now that they see what it was that they expressed, they say, "Well, that's not quite what we wanted." There's an interplay in the design process between their perception of what they really want and what they want, and that dynamic eventually comes out with their discovering what they want and revealing it to the architect. The architect doesn't tell them. The architect asks the right questions, he doesn't provide the right answers. They have to provide the answers.

I found Ackoff's description of who actually designs a vision somewhat confusing. He liked to say that the customer should design the product or service and the workers should design their work. In our discussion, he said, "But the same thing applies to work. Where the product is work, then the people who work have to do the designing of it, not a professional who claims to be an expert in the design of work." He then gave an example.

I had an experience recently that illustrates this. The workers were told, "You can do anything you want to do in your work groups providing it doesn't affect any other work group. If it affects somebody else, then you have to get their agreement."

One morning I got a phone call from the manager who is the vice president of production of this company. He said, "You got me into a terrible mess. One group on the shop floor decided they wanted to eliminate time cards and time keeping, and they called together all the other groups because it affected them. They all decided collectively that they want to eliminate all time keeping, and they say it doesn't affect anybody else except the people who are on the floor, and they informed me that they're going to make this change." He said, "I can't let them make it." I said, "Why not?" He said, "You realize there are certain machine sections down on that floor which if they're not manned shut down the whole factory." I said, "Yeah, I know that." He said, "If they don't man those machines, then I have a terrible loss. I've got to be sure that they're covered." I said, "Well, don't they know that?" He said, "Yeah. They know it." And I said, "What do you think they think you will do if you give them the right to eliminate time cards, and those machines are not covered some day?" He paused and he said, "I guess they think I'll go back to the old system." And I said, "Right. Then why do you think they suggested the new system?" And he said, "Well, I guess they think that won't happen." And I said, "Yeah. Right. Why don't you try it and see what will happen."

He called me about two months later and told me they had a 20 percent increase in productivity, down to 3 percent of the amount of grievances he previously had, and virtually no quality problems. He let them design the work, and the effect was tremendous.

This example is consistent with changes that occurred at Bolivar and Coatbridge. But they do not describe a process of changing a system. In our discussion, Ackoff went on to clarify that these kinds of changes needed to be integrated by the architect-leader, who would design a new system where all employees could participate in designing their work. Ackoff said,

> The executive who wants to change an organization has to start with the realization that the only thing that produces profound change is an idea. It seems to me that the basic idea the leader has to bring to bear is we're going to redesign this organization to enable you to have a say in what happens to you, to give you a stake in its outcome, and give you an opportunity to design what it is that you do within it. We have an obligation as an organization to serve your interests, as well as to serve the interests of the shareholders and the people outside.
>
> When he expresses all this and can convince the people who are below him that he means it, and he convinces them by what he does not say as well as by what he says, he can start the design process. He can get each unit within the organization to imagine that it has the opportunity to redesign itself from scratch. And then he can take these designs and try to mesh them together in the organization so that they fit each other. This becomes the inspiration that can produce profound change within the organization.

Ackoff proposed three criteria for designing a vision or idealized organization system by architect-leaders. They are:

- *Technological feasibility*—the design should not incorporate any technology not currently known to be workable. This does not preclude new uses of current technology. It is intended to prevent the design from becoming a work of science fiction.
- *Operational viability*—the organization should be designed to be capable of surviving in the current environment.
- *Learning and adaptation*—the organization should be designed so as to be able rapidly to learn from and adapt to its own successes and failures and those of relevant others. It should also be capable of adapting to internal and external changes that affect its performance and of anticipating such changes (foresight) and taking appropriate action before such changes occur. (Ackoff is describing a learning organization.) This requires, among other things, that the organization be susceptible to continual redesign by its internal and external stakeholders. The vision should be:
  - ○ designed by the leadership of an organization;
  - ○ communicated, understood, and shared by the organization. People need to see how changes would benefit them and other stakeholders. This requires that all parts of the organization participate in the interpretation, development, and testing of changes that lead to effective implementation of the vision;
  - ○ comprehensive and detailed—the vision should describe the organization as a system;
  - ○ presented with a time frame for actions that will move the organization toward the ideal future system.

Ackoff drew a picture of the change process toward an ideal future. It is presented in Figure 5.2.

The y axis measures results, however you want to define them. Leaders describe the system, or what Ackoff called "the mess" as it currently exists, and then design what it would look like today if it was producing the desired results. The x axis shows the years it will take to transform the current organization into the ideal system.

Ackoff left it to the leaders-architects to provide a method for designing the ideal system. And he did not describe the elements of an organizational system; he also left that to the designers. But all leaders are not gifted with the aesthetic sensibility Ackoff considered desirable for leaders of change. For change projects at AT&T, MITRE, and ABB, I decided that a conceptual model of a system would be useful. I used a version of the Seven Ss model of an

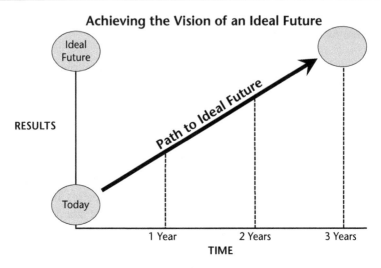

Figure 5.2. Achieving the vision of an ideal future

organizational system that was described by Richard Pascale and Anthony Athos in their enlightening study of Japanese management.[6]

Pascale and Athos contrasted American companies that, at best, integrated their strategy, structure, and systems—what they called the hard Ss—with the best Japanese companies, which add the soft Ss of skills, staff, style, and shared values.[7] Henry Ford was an example of a systems thinker who designed his company with the hard Ss. His strategy or purpose was to produce a car that most people could afford to buy. The structure was a prototypical Tayloristic industrial bureaucracy, with work roles on the shop floor shaped by time–motion studies that provided measurements (process systems) used by managers to coordinate and control work.

When Alfred Sloan became CEO of General Motors, he attacked Ford with a strategy that expanded the car market from Chevrolet that competed with the low-cost Ford up the quality-cost scale with Pontiacs, Oldsmobiles, Buicks, and Cadillacs. The strategy was to tie car ownership with moving up the status hierarchy. This strategy required a decentralized structure of companies headed by CEOs with profit-and-loss responsibility. The production systems were similar to those of Ford, but planning, human resources, and measurements were both centralized and decentralized.

In Japan, Pascale and Athos found that the hard Ss were integrated with the soft Ss, I saw this for myself when I visited a Toyota factory in Nagoya with a group of Volvo managers. For example, the Toyota values included leadership and innovation. The kind of leadership Toyota wanted from supervisors included teaching and facilitating collaboration. To develop leaders with these qualities, Toyota gave added pay to workers on the line who helped others and created group harmony. When it was time to select a supervisor, it was clear which workers had the qualities sought by Toyota. In contrast, Ford and GM promoted the best workers, not the natural leaders.

As for innovation, all workers were encouraged to offer ideas for improvement, no matter how trivial they might seem. An idea might be to change the placement of a tool, increase lighting, or move work offline. If the idea was accepted and improved productivity, the worker gained points that could be used to take a family to dinner or if many points were gained, a week's vacation in Hawaii. I asked the foreman who was showing me around how many ideas they were getting. "Fifty per person per year," he said. "That's amazing," I said, "an idea a week from each worker. How many have you used?" "Over 80 percent," and he added, "I've visited your factories in America. You give surveys to workers and you are happy when 80 percent state that they are satisfied. For us that would mean 20 percent have complaints that can be opportunities for improvement."

Systems thinking seems more natural to Asians than westerners. Taiwanese engineers complained to me that European engineers at ABB broke problems into elements while they started with the whole and its purpose before analyzing the elements. When I consulted to an auto parts factory in the US that made products for Lexus, Cadillac, and Mercedes, the chief engineer told me that when there was a quality problem, GM and Daimler demanded a quick fix, even if that added to cost. Toyota sent engineers who not only fixed the problem, but also did so in a way that improved the productivity of the system.

To teach systems thinking and provide a conceptual tool for systemic change, I used a modified version of the Seven Ss model (see Figure 5.3). Instead of "staffs," the meaning of which is covered by skills and style, I added "stakeholder values" to indicate that the organization's values should reflect the values of its key stakeholders, especially customers and employees, as well as owners.

1. *Strategy*—the predicted outcomes of productive work and the plans to achieve those outcomes in ways that meet shared and stakeholder values (strategy is an expression of purpose);
2. *Stakeholder Values*—the values of owners, shareholders, customers, and clients, constituents, strategic partners, etc.;
3. *Shared Values*—the values of employees, management, and leadership;
4. *Systems*—the processes and procedures;
5. *Structure*—the organizational roles, resources, relationships, and responsibilities;

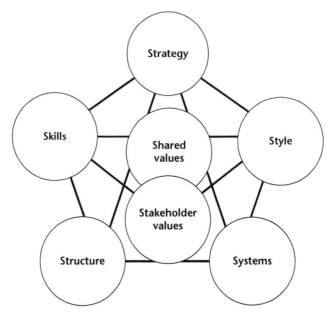

Figure 5.3. The Seven Ss

6. *Skills*—the capabilities of the workforce;

7. *Style*—the different ways of using skills productively and the style of leading.

The leadership teams I worked with described the current organization and then the ideal organization in terms of the Seven Ss. Different groups throughout the organization would then develop plans to transform the system, and leaders made sure that the changes interacted to move the system toward the idealized future.

During the past five years in leadership workshops, my colleagues and I have replaced the Seven Ss model with another conceptual tool, the Five Ps: purpose, product, practical values, people, and processes (see Figure 5.4).[8]

We define *purpose* and *practical values* as parts of organizational philosophy described in chapters two and four. Purpose substitutes for strategy. Practical values, more than shared values, emphasize the beliefs and behaviors essential to support the organization's purpose and create its offerings. *People* include the skills of employees and style of leadership consistent with values, purpose, and the *products* offered. And *processes* describe the organization of work and the systems used to produce products, motivative employees, and determine results. The products and services produced should express the organization's purpose. Processes will be different according to the products, as in ambidextrous organizations.

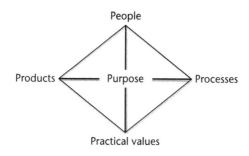

Figure 5.4. The Five Ps

Systems Metaphors

Using either the Seven Ss or the Five Ps models, Tim Scudder introduced the conceptual tool of *systems metaphors* in our leadership workshops. A systemic vision can be difficult to communicate to large groups of people. The use of verbal or visual metaphors can help people to understand the way the parts of a vision work together and fit into the larger view of the whole organization and how the organization functions in a larger system. Here are examples.

Unilever Corporation, one of the world's largest consumer products companies, has described its global business as a fleet of ships. Each business unit or brand is independent and strong, yet when working together as a unified fleet, they are even stronger.

A leader of an organization responsible for preserving a historic site identified a need for a change. Volunteers were plentiful, but volunteer time was not productive. The leader used an analogy of a harbor to communicate the change. The current harbor had the harbor master (volunteer coordinator) positioned on land, deep inside the harbor (the historic site), waiting for the boats (volunteers) to check in. The larger sea contained all the potential volunteers. The leader assessed that the biggest gaps in the Seven Ss model were in the areas of structure and systems. In the current harbor, there was disarray, with each boat doing its own thing independently or taking whatever slip or anchor position was most convenient. The future harbor was described as relocating the harbor master (volunteer coordinator) to the harbor entrance (which also involved a small shift in strategy to include more volunteer outreach), where each boat (volunteer) would be met, assessed, and guided to the best slip or anchor point (their volunteer task).

A financial services firm needed to inform several thousand people in the company about a multi-year information technology project that would change the nature of daily work. They created a picture of a team bicycle race to tell the story of the strategic change. Stakeholder values were represented by the crowd cheering for the racers (the people implementing the change). Known challenges were represented by mountains to climb (giving an opportunity to explain the strategy to address the challenges). Systems to feed the racers and maintain their equipment were made analogous to the support that would be offered during the change process. All seven Ss were represented in the picture.

An entire customer-focused strategy can be communicated easily to large groups of people using business models they interact with on a daily basis, such as a restaurant. Patrons (customers) have varying levels of needs for food (products) and expectations about their experience (service, entertainment, speed, customization, etc.). The restaurant needs to buy food (raw materials, products for resale, etc.), attract customers to get them to come back (customer retention strategies), create lunch and dinner menus (market segmentation), and many other functions, which may be made analogous to many types of organizations.

The use of metaphors, however, carries risks of over-simplification or extending an analogy too far. A metaphor of growing a garden, for example, may work on most levels, but would not address the needs of an organization to relocate the crops (products, clients, or whatever the crops represent in the metaphor) while they are growing. These limitations can be addressed in the analogy by taking creative license.

Interactive Planning

Designing and implementing a vision requires planning to describe the vision, determining the means to pursue it, locating the resources needed, and deciding who does what when.

Ackoff contrasted his view of interactive planning with conventional planning. He wrote that most planners just aggregate individual solutions to threats and opportunities. Ackoff applies systems thinking, starting with the whole and the interaction of its parts and then focusing on the parts. The planning process is best done interactively, engaging the whole organization as opposed to having it done by a group of expert planners at the top.

Ackoff compared interactive planning to three other types of planning in terms of their orientation to past, present, and future (see Table 5.2).

Reactive planners seek solutions to current problems in the past. Their first response to a problem is to look back to how things were before there was a problem. Reactive planning deals with problems separately, not systemically. An example of reactive planning might be when a company finds a product is losing money, top management cancels the product, and in so doing loses the business of some major customers who were among the few buyers of the product, but bought other products because they were compatible with the product in question. Unless planners view an organization as a system, they are likely to make mistakes like this that appear to solve a problem but actually damage the system.

Inactive planners want to keep things as they are. Like the Office of Circumlocution in Charles Dickens' novel *Little Dorrit,* their mission is to make sure nothing ever happens for the first time. Inactive planners muddle through. When there is a crisis, they do as little as possible to try to get back to where they were. An example of this is how GM and Daimler, in contrast to Toyota's systems approach, dealt with a quality problem.

Pre-active planning has been the approach most commonly practiced in large companies. Pre-active planners are future-oriented. They put considerable effort into forecasting, predicting possible futures. A professional planning staff predicts the future and top executives prepare a statement of corporate objectives and formulate a broad strategy for the organization. This is passed down to lower levels where lower-level objectives and programs are developed. Road maps for change are designed by the pre-active planners.

Typically, the planners at the top whose objectives are growth—to become bigger, increase market share, cover more countries—have very little interaction with lower levels of the organization. Middle managers would point to the executive offices on the fourteenth floor of the GM building and say "That's where the rubber meets the air."

Ackoff conceded that pre-active planning was better than nothing. It is important to foresee threats and opportunities and it is necessary to have objectives. But he believed that companies should focus more on creating their future, rather than adapting to a forecast. To design and move toward an ideal future, Ackoff argued that planning should be *interactive.*

Interactive planning builds on lessons of the past and deals with problems in the present in the context of designing the future. Continuity with the past is especially important for learning from experience and affirming organizational values. Our minds are always in the past, present, and future at the same time. When people have different views of the past, they have difficulty agreeing about the present and the future. I found this to be especially true when I facilitated an interactive design process with managers and union leaders. The managers focused on the future, the urgent need to change to meet increased competition. This included the need for the union to be more flexible about work rules. The union reacted to this by focusing on the past, the hard battles they fought to gain better work rules and benefits. Until both management and union participants understood each other's focus and concerns, it was impossible for them to agree on the challenges of the present and the need for change to meet the threats and opportunities of the future.

Table 5.2. The four basic orientations to planning

Orientation	Past	Present	Future
Reactive	+	−	−
Inactive	−	+	−
Preactive	−	−	+
Interactive	+/−	+/−	+/−

With the interactive planning process, everyone in the organization is engaged in moving toward the ideal. It is a kind of backward planning, but the goal is not necessarily to create the idealized future. By moving toward it interactively, the organization will also be able to innovate, and employees will develop their abilities. Employees are encouraged to experiment. The mix of products may change. It may even be necessary to modify the organization's philosophy. Objectives of interactive planning are learning and innovation, and the process should be fun as well as productive.

When we began interactive planning to develop the idealized design of ABB Canada from just producing products to producing products wrapped in solutions, key managers were enthusiastic about the process. They saw it as a way of better understanding each other and their customers and creating a common language. One manager noted that the interactive process was the best way to assure that the strategy would be understood throughout the organization. Another manager said, "Interactivity is the glue that makes the whole bigger than the parts." The managers predicted that the interactive process would continually develop and improve the strategy.

Building on Ackoff

Ackoff's conceptual tools of systems thinking, idealized design, and interactive planning have proved essential for leading change. But they are not enough. One of Ackoff's criteria for an idealized organization is its ability to learn from and adapt to its own successes and failures and those of relevant others, also to adapt to external and internal changes that affect its performance. These are attributes of a learning organization, but Ackoff does not describe how organizations learn. This requires processes. In our book, *Transforming Health Care Leadership*, we describe how the community health-care system in Jönköping, Sweden has regular meetings to share learnings.[9] We also report on a group of US healthcare organizations that share improvements in medical procedures and provide processes for physicians to suggest further improvements based on practice.[10]

Processes should also strengthen purpose and practical values. A learning organization requires processes that enable learnings from the frontline to reach the top of the organization and influence change. In his book, *Why Some Firms Thrive While Others Fail*, Thomas H. Stanton reports that the financial firms that made it through the financial crisis of 2007 had these processes, whereas those that failed did not.[11]

A learning organization does not just adapt; it involves all members in continuous improvement. The method favored by Deming is described in Chapter 8. Transforming a bureaucracy into a learning organization requires all the elements of what Deming termed profound knowledge. The idealized organization also needs a philosophy, understood by all collaborators. Furthermore, to implement an idealized design, leaders need to understand the motivations of collaborators, what engages and inspires them, and what causes resistance to change. This is discussed in Chapters 6 and 7. Ackoff was fully open to additions to his thinking; he was interactive in practice as well as theory.

Using the Five Ps to Design an Ideal Future

1. Describe your organization as it is today.
   a. What is the current purpose?
   b. What practical values support the purpose?
   c. What are the key processes, products, and services?
   d. What are the current roles and skills required by your people? How well are people being managed and motivated?
   e. What are the measures used to see how well the organization achieves its purpose?
2. Describe your organization in the future.
   a. Purpose
      1. What changes will be required in our purpose to describe your vision?
   b. Practical Values
      1. What changes will be required in your practical values to achieve your vision?
   c. Processes, Products, and Services
      1. What processes must be designed or redesigned to accomplish your vision and support the change?
      2. What products and services must be designed or redesigned to achieve your vision?
      3. What processes are needed for collaboration and sharing?

d. People
   1. What are the roles and responsibilities you need to fill and what kinds of people do you need to fill them?
   2. What are the skills they need to have?
   3. How should they interact? What are the important relationships?
   4. What kinds of interactions do you need to lead?
   5. How will work be evaluated and rewarded?

Notes

1. I am grateful to Clare Crawford Mason and Bob Mason for giving me a transcript of my conversation with Ackoff.
2. Russell L. Ackoff, *Creating the Corporate Future* (New York, John Wiley & Sons, 1981).
3. Russell L. Ackoff, *Creating the Corporate Future* (New York, John Wiley & Sons, 1981), p. 16.
4. Russell L. Ackoff, *Creating the Corporate Future* (New York, John Wiley & Sons, 1981), p. 16.
5. Russell L. Ackoff, *Creating the Corporate Future* (New York, John Wiley & Sons, 1981), p. 16.
6. Richard T. Pascale and Anthony G. Athos, *The Art of Japanese Management* (New York: Simon & Schuster, 1981). The Seven Ss model was also used and developed by Thomas J. Peters and Robert H. Waterman Jr in *In Search of Excellence* (New York: Harper & Row, 1982).
7. They referred to Alfred D. Chandler Jr and his analysis in *Strategy and Structure, Chapters in History of the Industrial Enterprise* (Cambridge, MA: MIT Press, 1962).
8. This is similar to Jay Galbraith's Star Model, a system that integrates strategy, structure, people, rewards, and processes. *Designing Organizations: An Executive Guide to Strategy, Structure and Processes Revisited* (San Francisco, CA: Jossey-Bass, 2002).
9. Michael Maccoby, Clifford L. Norman, Jane Norman, and Richard Margolies, *Transforming Health Care Leadership: A Systems Guide to Improve Patient Care, Decrease Costs, and Improve Population Health* (San Francisco, CA: Jossey Bass, 2013), p. 207.
10. Michael Maccoby, Clifford L. Norman, Jane Norman, and Richard Margolies, *Transforming Health Care Leadership: A Systems Guide to Improve Patient Care, Decrease Costs, and Improve Population Health* (San Francisco, CA: Jossey Bass, 2013), p. 41.
11. Thomas H. Stanton, *Why Some Firms Thrive While Others Fail* (New York: Oxford University Press, 2012).

6

Understanding the Personalities of Leaders, Followers, and Collaborators

The chief over-all function of personality, then, is to create a design for living which permits the periodic and harmonious appeasement of most of its needs as well as gradual progressions towards distant goals. At the highest level of integration, a design of this sort is equivalent to a philosophy of life.

—Henry A. Murray and Clyde Kluckhorn,
Outline of a Conception of Personality

The concept of social character does not refer to the complete or highly individualized, in fact, unique character structure as it exists in an individual, but to a "character matrix," a syndrome of character traits which has developed as an adaptation to the economic, social, and cultural conditions, common to that group.

—Erich Fromm and Michael Maccoby,
Social Character in a Mexican Village

As Russ Ackoff pointed out in our conversation reported in Chapter 5, I approach change by encouraging executives who see the need for change to be leaders. To do this, I have had to understand their values and interests, as well as their reasons for wanting change. The leaders I've worked with were not just motivated to increase profitability and win at the game of business. Some wanted to help their customers succeed and/or to improve working life for their employees. Others wanted to change the world for the better and be recognized for their achievement. I encouraged these executives to clarify and communicate their philosophies and act on their values. I helped them to understand themselves and the people they needed as partners and collaborators in change.

Understanding people, their personalities, and emotions, is an essential element of strategic intelligence; it enables partnering and motivating. Understanding others facilitates collaboration and avoidance of conflict.

This chapter presents the conceptual tools I've used to understand the personalities of people I've coached and worked with and the theories that explain these tools. These tools can be used to understand yourself, your partners, and other people you need as collaborators. Understanding the theory will help you to develop yourself and the people you lead.

Understanding People

Understanding another person requires both conceptual and emotional understanding, both head and heart. Conceptual knowledge of personality equips us to predict how a person will act, but it will not tell us if someone is angry, anxious, doubtful, or happy. To a limited extent, we can observe emotions in facial and bodily expressions.[1] However, a heart that listens combined with conceptual knowledge of personality equips us to make sense of what we both observe and experience in our interactions with others.

The behavior of people at work results from an interaction of personality, especially the person's motivational system of values and drives, and the workplace situation, including the challenges, relationships, and incentives. Understanding personality means being able to predict, with a high probability of success, how people will behave at work, how they direct their passions, and how they respond to challenges. Chapter 7 makes use of this understanding to present the methods and tools leaders can use to create an environment where people will be engaged and motivated to collaborate, to achieve a common purpose.

Psychologists have proposed many different definitions and theories of personality.[2] The *Oxford English Dictionary* defines personality as "the assemblage of qualities or characteristics which makes a person a distinctive individual." This definition can be improved by adding the Kluckhohn and Murray proposition that personality has the function of integrating these qualities and giving them meaning by developing a philosophy of life.[3]

Understanding and describing personality is an art. Compare the miraculous developments over the past 500 years in science and technology to advances in understanding people. Has our understanding of personality advanced from what we learn reading the works of Shakespeare, Cervantes, Charles Dickens, Jane Austen, Tolstoy, Balzac, and Mark Twain? Arguably, we've regressed. Shakespeare gave us characters we can use to describe key elements of a personality. "He's a Hamlet," describes a person who cannot make an existential decision. "She's a Lady MacBeth," describes a woman who will do anything to further her ambition. "He's an Iago," describes someone who betrays trust with destructive manipulations. Cervantes' Don Quixote is a prototype of an idealist on an impossible quest. Mark Twain's Tom Sawyer is a classical American entrepreneur who tricks others into doing his work. I can't think of current writers who have come close to equaling these incisive descriptions of prototypical characters.

Perhaps we have become less perceptive about people than we were in Shakespeare's time. In the peasant village I studied, people developed a perceptive rather than abstract intelligence that was adaptive to their environment. They were dependent on the weather, crops, and animals and were keenly aware of changes in all of those. They also sharply observed each other and shared their observations, noting attitudes of trust or distrust, friendliness or envy.[4] They had a relatively small number of people to observe and understand. They knew each other's strengths and weaknesses.

In the modern world it is much harder to understand the many people with whom we interact, often briefly, especially those raised in different cultures.

The Science of Personality

Freud, who often quoted Shakespeare, Cervantes, and other great writers, proposed a science of personality. During his career, he modified his theories of the forces driving behavior, but his approach to personality remained constant with these virtues:

- Personality is described as a dynamic system of forces vs a collection of qualities or a list of traits. This means that a quality can only be fully understood according to how it interacts with other qualities to achieve the system's purpose. A particular quality or trait may have different meanings and produce different behaviors in different systems. For example, aggressiveness may serve to dominate others or to protect them. The sexual drive may be linked to love or sadism.

- Personality is described as a system of forces that can be in conflict both internally and externally. For example, expressing an impulse can conflict with conscience (super-ego) or with expectation of punishment (ego). Someone's super-ego may repress an aggressive impulse, or it might be suppressed because that person fears aggression will be punished.

Based on his theory and clinical experience, Freud proposed different normal as well as pathological personality or motivational types. Subsequently, Erich Fromm, Elias Porter, and I have built on Freud's conceptual foundation in different ways. Personality types, which I'll describe later in this chapter, are one element of a broader understanding of personality.

The elements of personality include:

- *Instinctual drives*—how we are like all people;
- *Social character*—how we are like others raised in the same culture;
- *Motivational type*—how we are like some people within our culture (variations of social character);
- *Talents* and *temperament*—what we are uniquely given at birth;
- *Identity* and *philosophy*—how we integrate and give meaning to these elements, how we are like no one else.

Let's consider these elements.

Instinctual Drives—How We are Like All People

In *The Social Conquest of Earth*,[5] Edward O. Wilson theorizes that through natural selection humans are genetically programmed with two genes that may cause conflicting behavior. One is individualistic and selfish; the other is collaborative and altruistic. Psychological research indicates that we are all born with drives that can be directed either selfishly or collaboratively, depending on how they are shaped into personality and how we are led. Freud theorized that our drives develop through interactions with others into personality types. Building on Freud, Fromm described how society shapes human drives into a *social character* that facilitates adaptation to a culture, so that we want to do what we need to do to prosper materially and emotionally.

Fromm emphasized that personality types have both positive and negative potentials. They can cause us to be productive in work and relationships, or unproductive. Freud built his theory of personality with three drives: libido (sex), aggressiveness, and survival (ego drive). Fromm also used three somewhat different drives: survival, relatedness, and meaning. I have grouped the drives we all share into seven categories that build on Fromm's drives. Each of these drives can be developed into productive, value-driven, motivational systems or they can become addictions that drive us. In other words, they can either empower us or enslave us. If we develop these value-drives in a productive way that makes us stronger, consciously able to determine and satisfy our needs, we are then able to integrate these drives into our sense of self and develop a philosophy of life that guides our passions and decisions.

These drives, our intrinsic motivational systems, are triggered by emotions: pleasure, desire, pain, fear, shame, and guilt. Pride and hope, the expectation of a positive future, also trigger these drives. As we grow up, we can become aware of these drives as needs, and we can develop them by the decisions we make, the habits we form. Leaders can engage our drives by firing up emotions, such as hopes for glory or threats to survival. Our intrinsic motivations are energized by these drives, but as we'll see in Chapter 7, we are motivated when these motivational systems connect with our roles and relationships at work.

Seven Value Drives

These are the seven types of drives that become the emotionally charged needs and values that are shaped into our motivational value systems (see Figure 6.1):

1. *Survival* —we are driven to stay alive to gain sustenance, a livable environment (temperature, air), healthy rhythms of sleep and wakefulness, relief from life-threatening stress, avoidance of danger, and the means of defending ourselves by flight or fight. For many people in a rich society, worries about survival, focus not on getting enough to eat, but on maintaining health through diet, exercise, and relief of stress.

The human organism is quickly mobilized by real and imaginary threats to survival. When our survival drive is triggered, emotions of flight or fight and catastrophic images dominate thought and behavior. The possibility of uncertainty during change can alert the survival drive. Good leadership can bind survival anxieties by presenting a hopeful vision and directing people to act for the common good. The job of the leader throughout history has been to direct survival drives to common goals, to express and defend a vision that infuses followers with hope.

Figure 6.1. Seven value drives expressed as needs

This drive can connect with the drive for relatedness and develop so that we are moved not only to save ourselves, but to defend family, friends, and groups we identify with. However, the survival drive can become an addictive need for security, an anxious obsession with threats, real and imagined, that draws energy away from productive activities. The paranoid person is driven by fantasies and fears about survival.

2. *Relatedness*—babies need to relate to caregivers to survive. Psychologists of attachment theory show that the way babies relate to their mothers can shape future relationships. As we grow up, we need to relate to others to stay sane; the psychotic is emotionally isolated. As we develop, relatedness can become caring for others, helping them to develop, and being able to give and receive love. From early childhood, we have all sought to be understood and to be connected with other human beings. The drives for care, protection, and recognition inevitably clash with other more individualistic drives for autonomy, mastery, play, and dignity. The resolution of these conflicts depends not only on individual character, but also on the culture and its support for conformity vs individual expression.

In a Mexican village I studied, one of the most original potters suffered crippling anxiety because he was too original and feared being ostracized by the other villagers. In contrast, our society supports breaking away from constraining relationships to express the self. At an early age, we already react to excessive care as constraining. Paradoxically, we want to be free, but not lonely, so we seek playmates, work partners, or the camaraderie of a team. However, the drive for relatedness can become an addictive dependency need.

3. *Information*—this is the drive to gain sensory stimulation, messages (directions, cues, signals), feedback, knowledge, understanding. From early infancy, we seek information in the form of sights and sounds that exercise our faculties, and in reassuring messages. As we grow older, we need information to orient ourselves to the world we live in and avoid danger, find pleasurable experiences, and master skills. This ability to gather information from our environment is necessary to feeling human. Psychologists have found that putting a person into a dark, soundproof room disintegrates the individual's sense of self.

Culture and language shape the drive for information. In different cultures, people attend to and name the world according to their needs and traditions. Peasants notice and react to small differences in crops and animals, information that would not register in the urban mind. In peasant villages, information about neighbors—gossip—is highly valued as a form of social control. Today, gossip spreads by texting and social media. On TV and the Internet, people who follow gossip about celebrities experience a pseudo-sociability in the global village. In organizations, gossip becomes the main source of information when people lose trust in the messages coming down from the top.

All of us seek useful feedback, information that tells us how we are doing. People want to know the meaning of information. You cannot improve a score if you don't know what is being measured. Lack of information is troubling. People want to know plans so they can adapt. Yet some managers tend to hoard essential information and remain stingy with positive feedback.

As we grow, we acquire, store, and transform information more effectively to adapt to our environment and realize our aspirations. We learn to identify and solve problems and test hypotheses; we transform information into understanding, knowledge, even wisdom.

Managements often puzzle over how difficult it is to communicate information to the troops. Yet, when the message is trusted or appreciated, there is no communication problem. In a corporate building with 3,000 employees, the executive in charge worried about improving communication. But one winter day when an announcement was made at 2 p.m. that because of blizzard warnings, employees could leave early, the building cleared out within ten minutes. The problem was not a faulty process of communication but the credibility and usefulness of the message. However, the drive for information can become an unproductive addiction to information—for example, obsessively surfing the web or scrounging for bits of gossip.

4. *Mastery*—the need for achievement strengthens and develops the mastery drive. People are motivated by challenges that stretch but do not exceed their skills. But mastery requires some control over the job. Where the drive for mastery is frustrated at work, it may be expressed elsewhere or perverted. The corollary of Lord Acton's dictum that "power tends to corrupt and absolute power corrupts absolutely" is the equally certain law that powerlessness perverts. The drive for mastery can become a need for learning that develops our skills. Or, it can become an addictive need for control and power over others. It can drive micro-managing and bullying.

5. *Play*—this is the drive to explore, fantasize, find adventure, compete, experiment, innovate, and create. This drive might be grouped with mastery, since play can contribute to mastery by serving as a means of trying out new skills and strategies.[6] However, there is an important difference between play and other forms of mastery. Pure play belongs to the realm of freedom, while other forms of mastery are necessary to cope with the world. Play implies self-expression through exploration and invention. Only in its most developed forms does play merge with mastery to become creative work. That depends on disciplined technique necessary to express artistic and scientific discoveries with beauty and elegance.

Parents and teachers sometimes make children sacrifice play to mastery. Accommodation and conformity can dampen the spirit of play. When the drive for play is repressed, it doesn't disappear, but may emerge as mischief, or go underground as fantasy, escape to the canned creations of the media or to an inner, isolated world. Since free play is so individualistic, its development requires teaching that respects the unique individual or a temperament stubborn enough to resist regimentation. When the drive to play is not developed productively, it can become an addictive need to escape from reality into fantasy or compulsive gambling.

In the US and UK, the idea of making work into play has long been the ideal of entrepreneurs. The play spirit is a unique strength in these countries. It sparks a spirit of exploration, competition, innovation, and adventure. It provides a sense of fun and meaning to business people who enjoy making deals, marketers who play with product concepts, and researchers who test out hunches.

In the regimented workplace, people joke and play jokes as a form of rebellion. If this drive is engaged at work, people easily become motivated. People with the interactive social character described later in this chapter want more play at work, or work as play, and management that can provide it, at least some of the time, is rewarded with more engaged employees.

6. *Dignity*—this is the drive to gain respect, self-esteem, and for some people, glory. We must value ourselves to survive; our sense of dignity and self-esteem is essential to productive motivation. Notice the response of shame, pain, and anger when a young child is ridiculed. The drive for dignity appears fragile, easily crushed, but this perception is misleading. As adults, the pressures to survive or adapt may cause us to swallow humiliation. But while the drive for dignity may be frustrated, it is not extinguished, and takes another form. It is often perverted into revenge and hatred. This frozen rage of people at work can explode into destructive violence.

The demand for fairness and justice expresses the drive for dignity. At about age three to six, children recognize that others share the same feelings. The family and culture facilitate this emotion through teaching and games. Children learn to curb their egocentric drives and to respect the dignity of others. It is the role of parents and teachers to shame disrespectful children, not enough to humiliate them, but enough to ensure they learn good manners. Shamed in early childhood by a caring elder, children avoid being shunned later by a community that harshly punishes disrespect for others and the law. Plato and Aristotle argued that the capacity to feel shame made ethical development possible, since shameless people are beyond the reach of the moral community.[7]

Much human destructiveness results from frustrating the drive for dignity. Gandhi pointed out that people without dignity could not practice his nonviolent *satyagraha* (truth force).[8] They must first express their rage and either avenge their humiliation or overcome it through prayer. Gandhi became a model for maintaining dignity despite poverty, both in teaching and in the practice of a simple, self-sufficient way of life. However, the drive for dignity can dominate the personality. False pride, touchiness, the confusion of dignity with special privilege, the compulsive drive for approval, all these strivings for a sense of dignity undermine relationships.

In some people, the drive for dignity is so easily bruised that they compensate by over-defending it. For the Japanese, dignity is "face," and losing it can make life worthless. Machismo is an unending struggle to maintain an exaggerated sense of dignity. In the Washington DC inner city, young men have committed murder because they felt disrespected (dissed). In Latin and Islamic cultures, men express what seems like a caricature of touchy dignity compared to the English-speaking cultures, where playful and self-critical humor lightens up organizational life. Being able to laugh at our exaggerated need for dignity is a sign of emotional maturity. There is a universal appeal to Charlie Chaplin's silent ballets that deflated pompous people and created sympathy for the tramp's struggle to maintain dignity at the bottom of the social pyramid, even on the assembly line in the film *Modern Times*.

Success in the age of knowledge work requires attention to the dignity of both employees and customers. There is a notable lack of the service spirit in bureaucracies, and helpers in service jobs often feel like second-class citizens. Customers feel lucky to get help. Only if they can play the service role with dignity will service employees respect the dignity of customers. Wise leaders recognize the importance of respect for their associates.

7. *Meaning*—this is the drive that integrates the other drives and makes sense of our drives by infusing value in our strivings and behavior. All other needs are eventually shaped by the drive for meaning. It is the strategic drive. Although we may not be conscious of it, we give meaning to all our experiences and impulses. Even when we sleep, the drive for meaning shapes our dreams. Without meaning that gives hope, motivation dies. Emile Durkheim, the French sociologist, observed that extreme economic fluctuations that either wipe out people, making their struggles and hopes meaningless, or that deliver unearned windfalls, cause depression, resulting in higher rates of suicide.[9]

A large part of our identity is the meaning we create for our drives. We seek competence and knowledge to be good craftsmen or professionals. The drive for meaning turns other drives into values—for example, security, love, innovation, excellence. We clarify the meaning of our motivations by developing a philosophy of life, and in so doing we create our unique identities. A well-designed philosophy helps us to mediate our drives and values, to set priorities when they are in conflict. However, a compulsive need for meaning can cause us to become superstitious and put irrational meanings on events or impute meanings based on our fears or fantasies to every action or event.

	DEVELOPMENTAL DRIVE TO:	ADDICTIVE DRIVE FOR
SURVIVAL:	Protect	Security
RELATEDNESS::	Love and be loved	Care
INFORMATION:	Learn and understand	Novelty and stimulation
MASTERY:	Increase competence	Power over others
PLAY:	Explore and innovate	Escape, gambling
DIGNITY:	Be respected and respect	Praise, glory
MEANING:	Act purposefully	Certainty

Figure 6.2. Developmental vs addictive drives

These drives often merge, but they can conflict with each other. How these internal conflicts are resolved depends both on a person's philosophy and evaluation of the external situation. For example, the drive for survival, triggered by a threat to life, usually takes precedent over the drive for dignity or relatedness, but not always. Brave soldiers risk their lives to save their comrades, motivated by comradeship and honor.

Figure 6.2 summarizes the developmental and addictive expressions of these drives.

Genetic Differences in Expressions of Drives

Experience tells us that different people express these drives with different strength and intensity. There is some evidence for this in what psychologists call the Big Five personality traits, which have been shown to be largely determined genetically.[10] These five traits can affect the expression of a drive.

1. *Openness* or *curiosity* strengthens the drive for information.
2. *Agreeableness* facilitates relatedness.
3. *Conscientiousness*, determination, sticking with a task, versus being easily distracted, strengthens mastery.

4. *Emotional stability* or *resilience*, the ability to bounce back from emotional setbacks, strengthens the whole personality. The work of Salvador R. Maddi shows that resilience, although partly genetic, can be developed by training in what Maddi terms "hardiness." The training strengthens attitudes of commitment, control, and challenge.[11]

5. *Extraversion* versus *introversion* describes a cognitive style that may affect the expression of drives. Extraverts tend to be more expressive of thoughts and feeling, introverts less so. Of course, temperamental differences and talents also influence the expressions of our drives. People have different cycles of activity, different talents they want to express. But we all share the seven value drives and the need to shape ways of expressing them meaningfully.

Social Character: How We are Like Others Raised in the Same Culture

Social character is that part of personality shared by people brought up in the same way in the same culture or subculture. Our value drives are shaped by family, school, workplace, sports, and the media to adapt socially and economically to our culture, so that we *want* to do what we *need* to do to succeed.

Changes in social character follow changes in culture caused largely by transformation of the dominant mode of production. Of course, changes in social character may take time to catch up with culture change. People left behind whose social character cannot adapt tend to resist culture change. The social character of the most prosperous Mexican villagers was adapted to work that had changed little for centuries, not only there but also in villages throughout the world. The successful farmers were just like their parents and ancestors:

- self-sufficient and rooted in the land they farmed, hardworking, cautious, and conservative, with a strong sense of dignity based on independence and self-reliance;
- respectful themselves—they expected to be respected by others;
- used to the repetitive tasks of the seasons—they were patient as nature took its time to make their plantings grow, but also fatalistic, emotionally prepared for unpredictable calamities such as droughts and disease, shifts in market prices;
- often cheated by middlemen and politicians—they trusted only family members. A close-knit family with paternal authority reinforced by a religion made for a strong economic unit that provided security for the old as well as the young;

- used to making village decisions by consensus among the heads of family, mostly men but also some women.

Reading studies of peasants in other parts of the world and working with George M. Foster, the University of California anthropologist who was an expert on peasant life, I learned that the social character of these *campesinos* was typical for peasants in Latin America, India, China, and Eastern Europe. And the villagers' behavior conformed to what appears to be a general law about why free people want to follow a leader who pulls them out of their comfort zone. They will do so if they feel they need the leader to rid them of threats and oppression, or to help them get rich, in other words, conscious self-interest.[12] (Chapter 7 discusses why people follow organizational leaders.)

Bureaucratic Social Character

In the late nineteenth century, bureaucracies of industry and government began to dominate the economies of Western Europe and the US. In contrast to the peasant-craft mode of production, different personality qualities were needed for success in these modern bureaucracies. The people who worked in them—mostly men—had to fit into specialized roles in a hierarchy. They had to pass exams to get a job, and once hired, to follow rules and satisfy a boss in order to move up the bureaucratic ladder. The qualities required included expertise, precision, efficiency, and loyalty. Unlike the farmer whose timetable was determined by the sun and weather, the bureaucrat's schedule was determined by clocks.

Just as work was changing, so was family structure. In the typical bureaucratic family, the father went to work in an office or factory, and the mother stayed at home to care for the children and the house. Children were raised to identify with parents and their roles. This was the dominant type of family in Western Europe and the US until the mid-1970s. The school prepared children for bureaucratic careers, passing tests and pleasing the teacher to move up a grade.

The ideal boss at work was like a good father, a fair and caring autocrat. The few women who moved up the pyramid grew up with strong father attachments that they transferred to the boss.[13] The negative side of the bureaucratic social character is over-control, micro-management, and sadomasochistic relationships at work. Crudely stated, such bureaucrats are said to suck up and piss down.

Interactive Social Character

In the 1980s, as both workplace and family began to change, so did the social character. The new knowledge-service mode of production required an interactive social character that was naturally collaborative and open to constant change. Increasing global competition caused insecurity and the need for continual innovation in companies.

Besides the knowledge-service mode of production, the following factors have also been instrumental in shaping the interactive social character:

1. There are fewer two-parent homes with just the father working outside the home and more dual-career and single-mother-led households.
2. Children are sent at an early age to day-care centers, where they develop interactive skills and learn to depend emotionally on peers, so they are less emotionally dependent on parents.
3. There is early use of information/communication technology, and thus interaction with people around the globe.
4. Schools increasingly emphasize teamwork, as well as individual achievement. Leaders of knowledge work like Bill Gates are at the forefront of changing schoolwork to prepare children for knowledge work.
5. There is ready access to information on the Internet to challenge authority.
6. There is less trust of companies and less lifetime employment in one company. Employees expect to be free agents, seeking the best deal and frequently moving from job to job.
7. There is increased focus on continual learning to keep up with relevant new knowledge.

The interactive social character is both independent and collaborative. Interactives expect continual change. They are not loyal to companies, and do not expect companies to be loyal to them. They are adept at forming relationships, and also at dissolving them. They quickly make friends and build teamwork. They have learned to adapt their personalities, their self-presentation, to different situations and audiences.

Brought up in single-parent families, or families where both parents work, they are used to shared leadership. They are raised with democratic values, and they have no problem questioning or contradicting authority. They become expert at negotiating with parents, playing on parental guilt at not being at home for them. They see parents less as disciplinarians than as service providers who are concerned above all that they do well at school and activities that will prepare them for admission to college and for successful careers. They transfer this expectation on to managers.

At an early age, interactives become adept at using social and information technologies. At work, they are prepared to use these tools to innovate and solve problems. In contrast to bureaucrats, who evaluated their products in terms of excellence, interactives view value in terms of customer acceptance.

Interactives want transparent and fully credible leaders who treat them as collaborators, not followers. They only respect leaders who respect them, and who articulate and practice a meaningful philosophy. If they respect leaders, they are natural collaborators. However, they want to be able to continually develop their marketable skills at work, so that they remain desirable employees.

The negative side of the interactive social character is the lack of loyalty and lack of personality integration. They also have the tendency to devalue experience and overvalue themselves, to feel entitled because of their knowledge. Interactives may be connected to many people and related to few if any. They are so used to adapting to different situations, to wearing different masks, that they are in danger of losing their center, the person behind the mask.

Sherry Turkle, in *Alone Together: Why We Expect More from Technology and Less from Each Other*[14] illustrates a negative quality of interactives, the isolation of people who use their mobile devices for self-expression rather than conversation, connecting with others but not relating with them. On a visit to a family restaurant, you can often find a family sitting around a table and each member texting people not there. The expression on the woman in the photo in Figure 6.3 shows that relatedness has gone downhill as the man texts to someone not at the table.

Figure 6.3. Most connected and least related generation. Photo: author's own

Social Character vs Generation

Personalities are commonly typed by generation, not social character. People born in the early 1980s are called Millennials or Generation Y, following Generation X, brought up from the early 1960s to 1980. Brought up in a time of social rebellion for civil rights and against institutions and leadership, Generation X paved the way for innovations that have changed the social character. The usual description of Millennials is similar to the interactive social character. This is understandable, since the main factors shaping the interactive social character—the changing mode of work and family organization, information and social technology—began to emerge in the 1980s. However, all Millenials are not interactives. Many people born during this period have been raised in traditional homes and schools. Many are employees in bureaucracies where they are satisfied to work in traditional roles, with the possible difference that they are able to use the new technologies.

The mode of production and culture are in transition and so is the social character. Tim Scudder suggests the metaphor that generations are like waves, while the social character is the slower changing tide. There has not been enough time for all the effects of the changing mode of production, family, and schooling to fully transform the social character. We are in a transition period of social character, from a bureaucratic social character to the emerging interactive social character.

Many people in the less developed world have a farming–craft social character. And people with a bureaucratic social character find it hard to adapt to the knowledge-service mode of production. In workshops I've led, some people with a bureaucratic social character report that they feel pulled by their work to become more interactive.

Table 6.1 summarizes the three social characters: farming-craft, industrial-bureaucratic, and knowledge-interactive. The table connects the different

Table 6.1. Summary of three different social characters

	Farming–craft	Industrial–bureaucratic	Knowledge–interactive
Values	Responsibility	Stability	Continual improvement
	Independence	Hierarchy/autonomy	Independence/ collaboration
	Family loyalty	Organizational loyalty	Free agency/networking
	Sustainable production	Producing excellence	Creating value
Social character	Inner-directed	Inner-directed	Other-directed
	Identification with parental authority	Identification with parental authority	Identification with peers, siblings
	Hard working, hoarding, conservative	Precise, methodical, obsessive	Experimental, innovative, self- marketing
Socio-economic base	Independent farming	Market-controlling bureaucracies	Entrepreneurial companies
	Traditional technology	Slow-changing technology	New technologies
	Local markets	National markets	Global markets
	Uncertain weather and markets	Employment security	Employment uncertainty
	Extended family	Traditional family	Diverse family structures

socio-economic bases with the social characters and the values rooted in the social character.

Since 2008, I have given the questionnaire presented below (see Table 6.2) with statements that express bureaucratic vs interactive attitudes, to participants in leadership workshops and participants in the executive program, Consulting and Coaching for Change at the Oxford Säid Business School.

Write the number of your response to each statement in Table 6.3.

In each workshop, I have separated participants into three groups based on their bureaucratic-interactive scores: a predominantly bureaucratic group, a mixed group, and a predominantly interactive group. Each group has discussed the following conflict between interactive and bureaucratic types at work and has come up with a solution.

The interactive desire for quick increases in responsibility and authority is driven by an ideal of matching workers' talents to their work. The bureaucratic organization tends to advance people in steps or logical progressions based on the ideal of experience. Interactives tend to view bureaucratics as roadblocks and people who withhold opportunity; making interactives "pay their dues." Bureaucratics tend to view interactives as

Table 6.2. Social character questionnaire

How much do you agree with the following statements?

		Not at all	Very little	Some-what	Very much
1	It is important for me to have a clear role in my organization.	0	1	3	4
2	I'd like to work for an organization that values loyalty.	0	1	3	4
3	I can benefit from continual change.	0	1	3	4
4	I see myself as a free agent, alert to better opportunities.	0	1	3	4
5	I want to be part of a team of people who share the same values.	0	1	3	4
6	I work at continually developing myself intellectually, emotionally, and physically.	0	1	3	4
7	Leaders should be people with the most experience.	0	1	3	4
8	I care more that team members share a common purpose than that they have the same values.	0	1	3	4
9	I want to work in an organization that values seniority.	0	1	3	4
10	I am continually developing my network.	0	1	3	4
11	I want a job description with clear lines of authority.	0	1	3	4
12	I like to work in a team where leadership shifts to the person with the appropriate skills.	0	1	3	4
13	I like interacting with people throughout the world on the internet.	0	1	3	4
14	I prefer to be on a team where the leader is a facilitator rather than a boss.	0	1	3	4
15	I use the internet regularly to find information about people.	0	1	3	4
16	My goal at work is to meet the expectations set for me.	0	1	3	4
17	I care more that the work we produce is excellent than that it satisfies a customer.	0	1	3	4
18	The best boss is like a good father or mother.	0	1	3	4
19	I can change my image to fit the situation.	0	1	3	4
20	My goal at work is to be respected as an expert.	0	1	3	4

Table 6.3. Scoring of social character questionnaire

1 _____	3 _____
2 _____	4 _____
5 _____	6 _____
7 _____	8 _____
9 _____	10 _____
11 _____	12 _____
16 _____	13 _____
17 _____	14 _____
18 _____	15 _____
20 _____	19 _____
TOTAL:	TOTAL:
This is your bureaucratic score	This is your interactive score

Note: Tim Scudder ran correlation tests to determine whether construct and differential validity could be determined from scores of a sample of 438 managers and consultants. He found that all items that load to the bureaucratic scale are significantly correlated with the bureaucratic scale score and none of these items correlate significantly with the interactive scale score. Also all of the items that load to the interactive scale are significantly correlated with the interactive scale score. All of the items correlate more strongly with the interactive scale than the bureaucratic scale. This may be used as evidence to support the construct and differential validity of the interactive social character scale.

having an "entitlement mentality," wanting all the rewards and responsibilities without having earned them.

Typically, the bureaucrats resolve the conflict by educating the interactives about the importance of experience, showing them what they still need to learn, while interactives restructure organizations, placing people in roles that engage their skills and develop more collaboration. In contrast, bureaucratic structure seems to be hard wired in the mind of the bureaucratic social character.

Those in the middle, with both bureaucratic and interactive traits, are more flexible than the bureaucrats. Workshop participants from a large pharmaceutical company who were in-between social characters, concluded that they needed to recruit and satisfy interactives, because without them, they wouldn't develop innovative products. However, they suggested that bureaucrats could mentor young interactives about developing relationships within different parts of the company and with key customers. Some bureaucratic executives have built mutual mentoring relationships with technically smart young interactives. How well these relationships develop depend on how well these individuals with different social character understand each other.

Social Character and National Culture

I have worked in thirty-six countries, as a change agent, researcher, or teacher. I find that national culture influences social character, particularly in attitudes toward authority and collaboration. Some of these differences are significant. It is easier to gain consensus in Sweden than in the US, but once committed to change, Americans are more likely to try out new approaches without first seeking approval. Germans are more open to questioning each other, less afraid of conflict than Scandinavians. Social class makes a difference in developing relationships in the UK and also, despite their egalitarian ideology, in Sweden. Finns respect the leader who does not put on airs or distance himself from collaborators.

I could go on, but the main lessons I've learned about personality from working in different countries are:

1. The social character is shaped in every country to be adaptive to the dominant mode of production. There are major differences between people adapted to independent farming, bureaucratic industry, and knowledge-service work. This means that there are differences in social character within each country, and for the most part, they are greater than those of people adapted to the same mode of production in different countries. For example, peasants in Mexico and China are more alike than they are to bureaucrats or interactives in Monterrey or Shanghai. However, leadership and a strong organizational culture can modify the social character as described in Chapters 5 and 8.

2. Although national cultural differences affect the social character, because of globalization people in different countries who interact within the knowledge world are becoming more alike.

3. The best way to learn about national differences is to actively study them by asking questions, reading novels, histories, and guidebooks. I found people in each country who enjoyed teaching me about their national culture and who suggested books I should read.

4. In every society, people with the social character adaptive to their work are the most successful. Those with a social character that is not adapted will be frustrated and unsuccessful. In the introductory chapter of this book, we met a factory worker with a social character adapted to individualistic craft work and who suffered from the repetitive work and his loss of freedom. In the study of workers in a Tennessee factory, we found that workers with a farming-craft social character saw factory work as a necessary way of making money, but their intrinsic motivation was saved for farming and craft work. Workers with a more bureaucratic social character focused on moving up the organizational ladder to jobs with more opportunity and status.

I have learned that the same word can have different meanings in different cultures. For example, American executives typically say that integrity is an essential leadership quality. But by integrity, they mean honesty or having strong moral principles. That is the definition in the American editions of the *OED*. In the British edition, the meaning of integrity is closer to its Latin root, *inter*, something intact, uncorrupted. In Germany, I've heard the term used to describe acting according to one's principles, and in Sweden, integrity means owning one's space and not violating another's.

Motivational Type: How We are Like Some People in Our Culture

Fromm described personality types that he developed from Freud's examples as variations on the social character. He estimated that 50 percent of personality is the social character, 25 percent is personality type, and 25 percent is explained by genetic differences. He theorized that a particular type would fit best with a particular social character. Freud had proposed three main types that could be combined into seven mixed types.[15] The three types are:

- *Erotic type*—the main interest is loving and more particularly, being loved. This type is dominated by the fear of losing love and therefore especially dependent on others from whom they seek love.

- *Obsessive type*—this type has a strong super-ego and is dominated by the fear of conscience rather than the fear of losing love. Obsessives are inwardly rather than outwardly dependent. Freud saw this type as self-reliant and the "conservative pillar of civilization."[16]

- *Narcissistic type*—the chief interest is directed to self-maintenance. The super-ego is weak. These individuals are independent and not easily intimidated. They are aggressive and active. Freud wrote "People of this type impress others as 'personalities' and are particularly fitted to serve as support for others, to assume the role of leadership, to add new stimulus to cultural development or to attack the existing order."[17]

Fromm reinterpreted Freud's types as different ways of relating to the world to satisfy material needs and relate to others. He pointed out that each type can be more productive-active, self-directed, responsible- or unproductive-passive, reactive, conformist. He termed Freud's erotic type *receptive* with the positive quality of caring for others. The obsessive type was termed *hoarding* with positive qualities of patience, practicality, and tenacity and negative qualities of stubbornness and stinginess. The narcissistic type was termed *exploitative*, adding to Freud's positive qualities the negatives of arrogance, seduction, and exploitation.[18]

Fromm pointed out that the behavior of these types differed according to their social character. When Freud observed personalities in the early twentieth century, obssessives were the dominant type, the model for character development. This was because their personality type fit the social character formed in the era of craft and bureaucratic-industrial production. However, an obsessive farmer or craftsman who owned his own land or workshop was more independent than an obsessive bureaucrat who sought autonomy within the boundaries of his role.[19] As the mode of production and its cultural frame shifted to service, a new personality type emerged in response to its demands. Fromm termed this chameleon-like type the marketing personality. It has become the dominant personality type of the interactive social character.

The productive marketing type combines independence with interactivity, sharing, and collaboration. Flexible to the point of being protean, marketing types adapt easily to changing situations. I've described their negative traits in presenting the interactive social character: lack of a center, insincerity, and disloyalty. Like narcissists, marketing types lack a strong super-ego, because they don't identify strongly with parental figures. But in contrast to narcissists, who chart their own moral code, the moral code of marketing types is continually programmed and reprogrammed by groups they consider essential for their success. The effectiveness of a leader with a marketing personality depends greatly on the quality of the leader's close colleagues, since marketing types tend to form their views interactively, shaping them to what they think leads to success.

The usefulness of both Freud's and Fromm's types has been limited by the negative terms that made people feel judged. Elias Porter took Fromm's types, termed them motivational systems, and made them more accessible for people to use by emphasizing their positive qualities and renaming them with colors (see Figure 6.4). The receptive type became blue and was called *altruistic-nurturing*; the hoarding type became green and was called *analytic-autonomizing*; the exploitative became red and was called *assertive-directing*. The marketing type was called the *flexible–cohering* hub, based on Porter's scheme of mapping the types on a triangle. The three points are the extremes of the types, based on responses to Porter's questionnaire, and the hub is a circle in the center, representing a personality type that can make use of behaviors characteristic of the other types.

Porter, like both Freud and Fromm, stated that people can be combinations of types, and he provided descriptions of these combinations. His test has the virtue of showing how a person typically reacts under conflict, as well as when things are going smoothly.[20]

In *Narcissistic Leaders, Who Succeeds and Who Fails*,[21] I provide a questionnaire that elicits the Freud–Fromm types as leaders. I've termed the leadership types with their positive qualities: *caring*, *exacting*, *visionary*, and *adaptive*. (The negative versions are: dependent, obsessive, narcissistic, and marketing.)

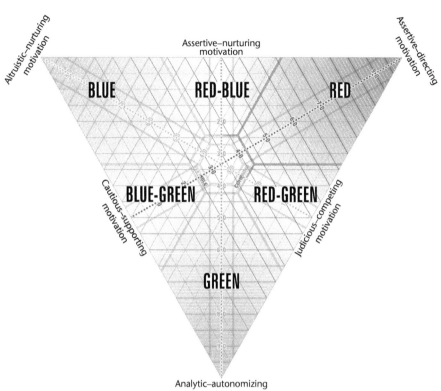

Figure 6.4. Porter Motivational System triangle

© Personal Strengths Publishing. Printed with permission. Scudder estimates that over two million employees of over 1,000 companies have taken the SDI questionnaires. There are now over 5,000 facilitators using SDI in North America, Europe, Asia, Africa, the Middle East, Latin America, Australia, and New Zealand.

The questions and responses used to determine these and the Porter types as well as the social character items have been shown to be highly internally consistent.[22] Tim Scudder, Gil Brady, and I have used my questionnaire in many workshops with consultants and executives, who have attested to the face validity of the types and have used them to reflect on their strengths and needs for development as leaders. This questionnaire, scoring, and description of typical leadership behavior is reproduced in the Appendix.

Consultants and executives who are dominantly caring see themselves as helpful and trusting, but they avoid conflict, don't stand up for their views, and tend to be overprotective. The exacting types see themselves as loyal with high standards, but they admit to getting lost in details, to micro-managing, and resisting change. Visionaries see themselves as passionate, competitive, persevering, and charismatic. But they admit to not listening to others, impatience, and arrogance. Adaptives see themselves as adaptive, self-starters, natural network leaders who want to make work playful. They admit to being indecisive and disloyal.

These types are essentially motivational systems that integrate value drives. Although we share all the drives, differences in upbringing and experience result in different patterns of these drives, with different drives dominant in each type: for the caring or altruistic-nurturing type, relatedness; the exacting or analytic-autononizing type, mastery; the visionary or assertive-direction type, a combination of survival, mastery, and dignity or glory; the adaptive or flexible-cohering type, a flexible ability to adapt different combinations of drives to the situation.

The Value and Limitations of Personality Types

We don't see what we don't name. By naming personality types, we become sensitive to patterns of behavior. When we understand a person's motivational values system, we are better able to relate to him or to her. We are better able to collaborate and to avoid conflict. By understanding our own personality type, we are better able to manage and develop ourselves. But each of us is unique; personality types do not describe the whole person.

Can people change their type? Since we are all a mix of types, changes in a person's situation can strengthen or weaken a particular drive. This may be caused by a change of work role or a change in family role. Erik Erikson described the psychosocial challenges at different stages of the life cycle. How we resolve these challenges—such as becoming independent, developing competence for the workplace, creating a family—shapes our personality.[23] In the *Leaders We Need, and What Makes Us Follow*, I describe the differences in these challenges in forming bureaucratic and interactive social characters.[24]

Questions about Your Personality Type

1. How would you describe your personality type or motivational value system? Take the questionnaire in the Appendix and compare the results with your description.

2. What are your strengths?

3. What qualities get in the way of your effectiveness?

4. What are you doing or should you be doing to develop your strengths, accentuate the positives, and eliminate the negatives?

Questions about the Personality Types of a Partner

1. How would you describe your partner's personality type? Ask your partner to take the questionnaire and compare the results with your description.
2. What are your partner's strengths?
3. What qualities get in the way of your partner's effectiveness?
4. How do your personalities affect your relationship? How can understanding of personality improve the relationship?

Identity and Philosophy of Life

Our motivational value systems also include the drive to give meaning to our motives and striving. How we do this becomes our identity or philosophy of life.

Identity and Philosophy: How We are Like No One Else

There are different meanings of identity, representing levels of individuation (see Figure 6.5). We may combine any or all of these meanings in our identities. At the most basic level, our identity is a combination of our physical traits—sex and race—and the social context we are born into—family, tribe, religion, and nation. In times of danger, people may trust only those who

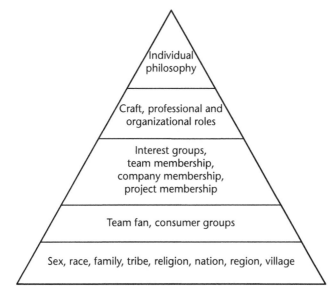

Figure 6.5. Levels of identity

107

share a tribal, religious, or national identity: Sunnis vs Shias in Iraq and Syria, Protestants vs Catholics in Northern Ireland, Israelis vs Palestinians.

The second level, identity based on supporting a team or identifying with a consumer group (e.g. cars, motorcycles), requires choice. The third level of identifying with an interest group (e.g. political party, trade union, organization) requires a bit more commitment. The fourth level of identifying with a craft (e.g. carpenter, electrician) or a role in a company (manager, executive) indicates pride in achieving a respected status. And the highest level of identity formation is the integration of our values, the development of a philosophy of life. At this level, religion is no longer just what we have been born into, but a transcendent belief system we have integrated into our personal philosophy.

We can't avoid being identified by our physical characteristics. As we age, our identity shifts with our role in life, from child to grown-up. We may become a husband or wife, parent, and grandparent. We shift from a student to a work-related role. Craftsmen and professionals have traditionally identified with their trades, and their identities are all affirmed by their associations.

In the peasant village, people's identities were very similar to those of their parents, grandparents, and ancestors back in time. Their identities were formed, essentially, by identifying with their work, family, and village.

In the bureaucratic-industrial age, people began to identify with companies that gave them status and life-long employment. Some identified with a union that protected their interests at work. As people begin to move away from their place of birth, they identified with a state, region, and country.

Of course, people still identify with family, religion, and region. But people with an interactive social character have flexible, less sticky identifications. They are less likely to accept identities given to them and more likely to express those spiritual, emotional, sexual, and cultural identities they have forged for themselves. However, they may identify with a project, rather than a company, an avocation (sport, musical group), rather than an occupation. They easily move from identifying with the team they used to play for, to the team they now play for.

What Leaders Should Know About Identities

A leader should know the identifications of followers and what those identities mean. However, these identifications can be misleading. For example, the identity of "Hispanic" in America may be shared by descendents of original Spanish settlers, Salvadorian farmers, Cuban professionals, and third-generation immigrants who don't even speak Spanish. It doesn't mean that all who identify themselves as "Hispanic" share cultural traits, but it may mean that they share the interest of gaining special consideration at work or political representation.

Respect people's identifications, but don't assume that people with the same identities share values and personality. The most effective leaders are able to stimulate members of a group to share an identity. This strengthens collaboration and motivation for group success. This is another reason for developing a leadership philosophy that can be shared by members of a group.

Now, consider the highest level of identity: our personal philosophy, what we commit ourselves to do and not do. In the peasant village, everyone knew what to expect from each other. If villagers did not follow the group moral code, they were ostracized. In our diverse and constantly moving world, we won't even know ourselves unless we become aware of our drives and values, and shape them according to our beliefs about who we ought to be and what we stand for. Then, we'll know ourselves, and others will be able to know and trust us.

William James in his essay *Pragmatism*[25] wrote that we all have a philosophy, but many people are not aware of their philosophy. Our philosophy includes our purpose in life and the values that support that purpose. For some people, this philosophy has been programmed in childhood. The purpose is just getting ahead or reaching some goal, such as a place on the occupational ladder or some amount of money. The values include doing what is needed to achieve that goal, relating to people who can help, and doing the necessary work. Others have chosen a purpose that includes a loving relationship and meaningful work that engages their talents and values and contributes to the wellbeing of others.

Models of Personality

There is no fully satisfying way of charting the elements of personality. Freud in *The Ego and the Id*[26] drew a structural dynamic model, with these interacting parts:

1. the id, the source of unconscious drives and passions;
2. the super-ego, composed of partly unconscious moral commands programmed by parents in childhood and conscious ideals and values shaped by identifications with admired people (ego ideal);
3. the ego, based on perceptions of the external world, which "has the task of bringing the influence of the external world to bear on the id and its tendencies, and endeavors to substitute the reality-principle for the pleasure-principle which reigns supreme in the id . . . The ego represents what we call reason and sanity, in contrast to the id which contains the passions."[27] The ego is connected to our perceptual mechanism that acquires and transforms data to information. Part of the ego is pre-conscious, meaning it can be brought to consciousness while another part remains unconscious because id impulses and ideas have been repressed as dangerous.

Freud's model (see Figure 6.6) assumes that a person's purpose is to maximize pleasure. But this is only a partial purpose of personality. I have constructed an alternative model that integrates the elements presented in this chapter. The purpose of this system is not limited to pleasure. It includes a range of meaningful activity including work, play, and good relationships that set one on a path to happiness.

In my model, the ego's reasoning, its response to challenges perceived and internal drives, are determined by intellectual and emotional abilities interacting with values, identity, and philosophy. The drives, the emotionally charged motivational systems we are all born with, are shaped and developed first in the process of socialization, then by our conscious efforts to strengthen the values that fit our ideals and philosophy. Social character influences the whole system of personality, including how we perceive the world (see Figure 6.7).

We should keep in mind that our reasoning combines the intellect and emotions, the head and heart. What we decide to do is shaped by our identity

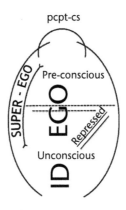

Figure 6.6. Freud's personality system

From "Dissection of the Personality," *The Standard Edition of the Complete Psychological Works of Sigmund Freud*, Vol. XXII (1932–1936) (London: The Hogarth Press 1932), 78.

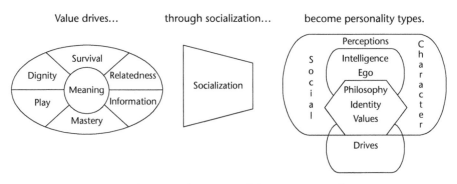

Figure 6.7. Transformation of drives to personality

and values, as well as our judgment about the best course of action. Our conscience, the quality that determines our moral behavior, is not only a super-ego programmed in childhood but, as Fromm points out, we can develop a humanistic conscience, a heart that listens. It can be as hard or harder to know ourselves as to know others.

The Personality Toolbox

In this chapter, we have explored the elements of personality. Few leaders will become experts in understanding others, but the chapter has presented basic tools that can be used for understanding:

- what motivates people at work—results of the social character questionnaire and tools such as the Strength Deployment Inventory (SDI) or the questionnaire in the Appendix can be shared and discussed by groups at work. My colleagues and I have facilitated this process many times and the results have always been an improvement in relationships.

- what is needed to understand partners and close collaborators—besides the tools mentioned above, partners should share their personal philosophies and discuss how their philosophies support the organization philosophy. They should consider how their personalities work together. What are their combined strengths? What are possible conflicts, and how can they be avoided?

- what is needed to understand and develop yourself. Consider the following:

1. Describe your personal philosophy, including your purpose in life and the values essential to achieve that purpose.

2. How does this philosophy compare to the leadership philosophy you described at the end of Chapter 4? Are they consistent? If not, what do you need to change?

3. How well are you practicing your philosophy? Is there anything you would like to change? If so, how will you begin to do so?

Personality and Freedom

To conclude this chapter, although our personalities are in part genetically programmed and in part shaped by early experiences, we can develop our personalities. At different stages of life, we face psychosocial challenges, such as succeeding at school and the workplace, achieving intimacy, taking a mentoring role, and becoming a leader.[28] We can meet these challenges by being more self-aware, freer to shape and satisfy our needs, to give new meanings to our drives, and to clarify our philosophies. We can become more productive at work and loving in our relationships. This may require frustrating addictive needs and practicing more productive behavior by reinforcing new habits, consistent with our values. Leaders are often advised: "be yourself." This means being authentic, expressing your philosophy not only in words, but also by deeds. And in the process of developing and practicing a philosophy, we are creating ourselves.

Notes

1. Paul Ekman, *Emotions Revealed: Recognizing Faces and Feeling to Improve Communication and Emotional Life* (New York: Times Books, 2003).
2. For a discussion of these different theories, see Salvatore R. Maddi, *Personality Theories, A Comparative Analysis*, 6th edn (Lions Grove, IL: Waveland Press, 1996).
3. C. Kluckhohn, and H. A. Murray (eds), *Personality in Nature, Society, and Culture* (New York: Alfred A. Knopf, 1953), p. 32.
4. Michael Maccoby and Nancy Modiano, "On Culture and Equivalence," in Jerome S. Bruner, Rose R. Olver, and Patricia M. Greenfield. (eds), *Studies in Cognitive Growth* (New York: Wiley, 1969).
5. Edwin O. Wilson, *The Social Conquest of Earth* (New York: Liverrights, 2012).
6. Jean Piaget, *Play, Dreams and the Imitation in Childhood* (London: Heinemann, 1951).
7. Plato, *Laws*, II, 671, trans. B. Jowett (Princeton, NJ: Bollingen Foundation, Princeton University Press, 1973); Aristotle, *Nicromacheon Ethics*, IV, 9 (Indianapolis: Bobbs Merrill, 1962).
8. Erik H. Erikson, *Gandhi's Truth* (New York: W. W. Norton and Co. Inc., 1969), pp. 184, 197, 207ff.
9. Emile Durkheim, *Suicide: A Study in Sociology*, trans. J. Spaulding and G. Simpson (Glencoe, Il: The Free Press, 1951).
10. See, for example, Paul T. Costa, Jr and Robert R. McCrae "Trait Psychology Comes of Age," in John J. Berman and Theo B. Sondereger (eds), *Psychology and Aging: Nebraska Symposiums on Motivation*, vol. 30, 1991 (Lincoln, NB: University of Nebraska Press, 1992), pp. 169–204.
11. See: <http://www.hardinessinstitute.com> (accessed November 2014) and Salvador R. Maddi, *Hardiness, Turning Stressful Circumstances into Resilient Growth* (Heidelberg/ New York/London: Springer Dortrecht, 2013).
12. This description of peasant social character is taken from my book, *The Leaders We Need: And What Makes Us Follow* (Boston, MA: Harvard Business School Press, 2007).
13. Margaret Henning and Anne Jardim, *The Managerial Woman* (New York: Anchor Press/Doubleday, 1977).
14. New York: Basic Books, 2011.
15. Sigmund Freud, "Libidinal Types," *The Psychoanalytic Quarterly*, 1(3–6) (1932): 3–6.
16. Sigmund Freud, "Libidinal Types," *The Psychoanalytic Quarterly*, 1(3–6) (1932): 4. In 1908, his earliest writing on character formation, the predecessor to the obsessive

type, was the anal character. Freud described qualities of extreme cleanliness, obstinacy, and stinginess as reaction-formations or defenses against the desire to gain pleasure from anal eroticism. By 1932, his theory had evolved, with a greater emphasis on the role of interpersonal relationships in the formation of personality.

17. Sigmund Freud, "Libidinal Types," *The Psychoanalytic Quarterly*, 1(3–6) (1932): 4.

18. Erich Fromm, *Man for Himself* (New York: Rinehart and Company, 1947), pp. 114–15.

19. Michael Crozier, in *The Bureaucratic Phenomenon* (Chicago, IL: University of Chicago Press, 1964) shows the French bureaucrat defending autonomy by sticking to the rules and resisting invitations to participate.

20. Tim Scudder and Debra Lacrois, *Working with SDI, How to Build More Effective Relationships with the Strength Deployment Inventory* (Carlsbad, CA: Personal Strengths Publishing, 2013).

21. Boston: Harvard Business School Press, 2007.

22. See Appendix for measures of internal consistency.

23. Erik H. Erikson, *Childhood and Society* (New York, W. W. Norton & Co, 1950).

24. Michael Maccoby, *The Leaders We Need and What Makes Us Follow* (Boston, MA: Harvard University Press, 2007). See Appendix.

25. William James, *Pragmatism* (Cambridge: Harvard University Press, 1975 [1906–7]).

26. Sigmund Freud, *The Ego and the Id* (London: The Hogarth Press, 1947), p. 29.

27. Sigmund Freud, *The Ego and the Id* (London: The Hogarth Press, 1947), p. 30.

28. Erik H. Erikson, in *Childhood and Society* (New York: Norton, 1950), described how we develop our personalities and identities as we respond to the psychosocial challenges of the life cycle. In the Appendix of *The Leaders We Need*, I contrast the different responses to these challenges by people with bureaucratic vs interactive social characters (Boston, MA: Harvard Business School Press, 2007), pp. 191–211.

7

Smart Motivation for Change

Motivation: The (conscious or unconscious) incentives, motives, etc. for actions toward a goal . . . the factor giving purpose or direction to behavior.

—*Oxford English Dictionary*

For me happiness is about finding a job that I love and enjoy doing every day with the fullest of energy.

—Claire, a twenty-four-year-old woman applying
to be a volunteer at Nuestros Pequeños Hermanos
(a home for orphaned and abandoned children)

Russell Ackoff had no use for surveys of worker satisfaction. He said the only useful survey would ask one question: "If you had all the money you'd need to live comfortably, would you still return to your job?" If the answer was "no," there was something wrong with the job for that person. This is an extremely demanding test of motivation, but Ackoff was dramatizing the view expressed in the quote from Claire. Money alone may motivate someone to stay in a bad job, but it does not motivate someone to do a job with the fullest of energy. It does not cause people to become engaged in the sense that they care about their work and take responsibility for results. Yet leaders of change need people with this kind of engagement and motivation to implement a vision (see Figure 7.1). What can leaders do to gain engaged and motivated collaborators?

An example of a company with engaged and motivated employees is C. B. Fisk, the leading builder of organs for churches and auditoriums throughout the world. There are about thirty craftsmen and women employed. Their craft work ranges from a medieval process of shaping pipes to a high-tech programming of software for consoles.

Virginia Stone, Chairman and CEO emeritus took me on a tour of the factory and introduced me to some of the craftspeople. I asked one man if I could ask him a personal question and he told me to go ahead. Would he continue to work at C.B. Fisk if he had all the money he needed? He thought about it and said, yes,

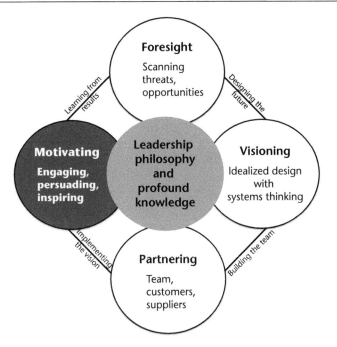

Figure 7.1. Strategic intelligence highlighting motivation

but he'd probably work fewer hours. I asked what he liked about the work. He liked the freedom to work at his own pace, building a product of the highest quality. He liked having his ideas listened to. He also liked the idea that people would be enjoying the music played on the organ he was building.

I learned that building a great organ requires both individual craftsmanship and collaboration. Employees help each other, not only at work, but when someone needs help in moving to a new house. The founder, Charles Fisk modeled his style of leadership after the team of physicists he worked with on the Manhattan Project that produced the first atomic bombs. He began the practice of involving his collaborators in day-to-day decisions about the concepts and construction of the instruments. Workers who offer innovative ideas are recognized and rewarded. Workers also hold shares in the company.

In this chapter, we will see that what engages and motivates a Fisk organ builder are the elements of *smart motivation* that can be applied in many organizations.

Theories of Motivation

Ideally, leaders recruit people who are intrinsically motivated to do the jobs the leader needs done. Even with such people, leaders need to provide

115

opportunities for them to find roles that connect with their values and skills. Furthermore, leaders need to strengthen their motivation with the conceptual tools that will be described in this chapter.

There are many theories of how to motivate people at work. They essentially fit into two buckets: hard and soft theories. The hard theories advise using measureable incentives, carrots and sticks: money, promotions, and threats. If workers meet performance standards, they keep their jobs, and if they exceed standards, they are paid more or promoted. These incentives can motivate people who are working at a job that does not engage their intrinsic motivation, such as repetitive tasks on an assembly line. Money motivates those stock and bond traders who would be doing something else if their jobs did not promise lots of money. Money can motivate. It can also attract people to take a job because of the pay and benefits.

Money can also distort behavior, impede innovation, and even demotivate people. Someone who hopes for a bonus may be motivated to please the boss at the expense of withholding ideas or information that would contradict or displease the boss. People competing for a limited pot of money are not likely to collaborate. Once people expect a bonus, they may be turned off when they don't get it.

Fear can be a motive to collaborate, but only when it's to fight an enemy. Facing resistance by workers who were not invited to participate in the re-engineering of their jobs, Michael Hammer, the guru of re-engineering, wrote "You must play on the two basic emotions: fear and greed. You must frighten them by demonstrating the serious shortcomings of the current processes, spelling out how drastically these defective processes are hurting the organization."[1] Most of these re-engineering change projects failed, including some I observed at AT&T. When people are fearful, they may comply, but they don't take the initiative. You will never drive out all fear from hierarchical organizations. People are wary of bosses who can hurt them. But by increasing fear you will squash any chance of creating a learning organization.

Soft Theories

In the 1950s, Harry Harlow, a professor at the University of Wisconsin, reported that monkeys learned to solve problems that appeared to be interesting challenges for them.[2] But when Harlow rewarded the monkeys with bananas for solving a problem, such as opening the lock on a door, their performance deteriorated. Harlow was showing that fully fed and secure animals are intrinsically motivated to solve problems. There was no need for incentives other than an interesting challenge. Rewards, extrinsic motivators, confused them. Rather than the enjoyable task of problem solving, where they were in control, the monkeys started working for bananas, over which they had no control. For monkeys, there is intrinsic motivation to solve problems. And so it is for human beings.

Harlow's finding, supported by a number of experiments with humans, shows that performance at an interesting task is better when there are no material rewards.[3] This finding is especially relevant for professionals and knowledge workers who have interesting tasks. Money does not motivate most professionals to do a better job. Good doctors do not treat patients better if promised more money. Good teachers will not teach better in order to gain a bonus, but they might teach to a test, if that is the basis of their pay. People with a job they love will not be more motivated to do good work by money, but they will be resentful if not paid fairly for their work.

Would they be more motivated by the application of a soft theory? One soft theory proposes that people are motivated to produce more for caring leaders. This was the theory proposed by Elton Mayo, based on the famous Hawthorne experiments at a Western Electric factory in the 1930s. Clearly, people prefer a caring boss, and many of the most capable employees leave companies because they dislike an autocratic or uncaring boss. But a caring boss is not a substitute for work that engages intrinsic motivation.[4]

Another suggestion from the soft theorists is to give people autonomy. Traditionally, bureaucrats have wanted autonomy, freedom from micro-managing bosses, and Peter Drucker responded by proposing Management by Objectives (MBO), directing bosses to give subordinates objectives and then letting them determine by themselves how to reach them.[5] Recently, Daniel Pink has sermonized in lectures and print that autonomy is the royal road to employee engagement. He writes: "The way that people engage is if they get there under their own steam, and that requires sometimes enormous amounts of autonomy over people's time (when they do what they do), over their technique (how they do it), over their team (who they do it with) and over their task."[6] Pink's example is from a software company where technicians are given free time to innovate. Autonomy can be especially motivating when innovative people can make work into disciplined play. But clearly, all employees are not equipped to go off by themselves to innovate, and autonomy does not motivate people to collaborate in change. Google experimented by giving employees a day a week to innovate, but gave up the experiment because of poor results.

When I first led the change projects described in Chapter 1, I was guided by Einar Thorsrud, who believed that if workers had a say in decisions affecting them, their jobs would be more interesting and they would become engaged and motivated. This worked well for some people but not others. A group of women on an assembly line resisted attempts to engage them, including "enriching" their jobs, meaning making the job more complex and with more autonomy. When asked why they rejected attempts at soft motivation, they told us that their work had become almost automatic. They did their jobs without thinking, so they were free to talk to each other, to learn the latest gossip, or share news about their families. The factory was in farm country, and these women with farming-craft social characters took factory jobs only to supplement insecure farming income. Their intrinsic motivation was saved for homemaking, childrearing, and craft work like making clothes and preserves.

It might have been different during wartime. During World War II women replaced men in factories making equipment for the battlefield. According to studies reported at the University of Nebraska, "Women were motivated not only by patriotism and the drive for high wages, but by the sense of community they gained in from participation in a huge undertaking."[7] The reason for working, winning the war, engaged their intrinsic motivation. It was meaningful.

There is no one way to engage and motivate people at work. To gain collaboration for change, you need to understand personality and create a motivating culture that integrates elements of hard and soft theories into what I call smart motivation.

Smart Motivation

Understanding how to employ the conceptual tools of smart motivation is part of strategic intelligence. It is the ability to make use of the Five Rs: *reasons, responsibilities, recognition, rewards,* and *relationships* (see Figure 7.2).[8]

Here are the Five Rs and their relationship to the intrinsic motivation of different personality types.

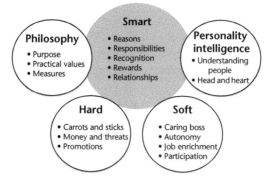

Figure 7.2. Motivation: hard, soft, smart

- *Reasons*—people are motivated to support change when the reason for that change, consistent with the organization's purpose and values, makes them proud (self-esteem, dignity) of work that connects to their values. Caring people are especially motivated by opportunities to help others or improve their lives. Exacting people feel pride in quality work. Visionaries are motivated by work that changes the world. And adaptives are especially motivated by work that customers and colleagues consider valuable.

- *Responsibilities*—people are motivated by challenging responsibilities, work that engages their skills and values. Caring people are especially motivated to teach others or to care for people in need and also to provide customers with good experiences. Exacting people are particularly motivated in jobs that make use of their skill to solve problems, build products, design systems, and improve efficiency. Visionary people are, of course, motivated to realize their visions. Adaptive people are motivated to exercise their interactive skills in teamwork that creates value for customers, develops their own capabilities and marketability, ideally, with playfulness. This may include freedom to explore and test their ideas.

- *Recognition* for contributions strengthens dignity (self-esteem) for all personality types. We all want to be recognized for contributions that lead to improvements. But when bosses take credit for our contributions, we are likely to become angry and demotivated.

People respond especially well to recognition that connects to their values. Caring types respond especially well to appreciation. Exacting types prefer certificates and plaques they can hang on the wall that recognize significant accomplishments, such as passing courses or becoming black belts in a six-sigma quality program. Visionary people seek the glory of having done the impossible. And for adaptive people, the most motivating recognition is new assignments that promise to increase their knowledge, skills, and marketability.

Recognition is a powerful motivational tool that is seldom used enough. Jane and Cliff Norman, who have consulted to change projects in the US, Canada, Europe, and Singapore suggest three reasons why recognizing contributions to improvement is not only motivating, but also supports change from a bureaucracy to a learning organization.

1. When the leader of a team is the only person who is recognized for a project's success, those who have contributed feel that their contributions were not so important or appreciated. This often happens when improvement experts (e.g. black belts, master black belts, and improvement advisers) are recognized but the people essential to their success are

not. When people who contribute are recognized, they are more motivated to participate in other projects.

2. Leaders who take the time to listen to team members as they tell their story, including failed predictions and tests, motivate people to keep trying to innovate.

3. Good examples should be published so that others can learn from them, and people should be recognized for their contributions to these examples.

Other ways that teams and individuals who have contributed to significant improvement efforts can be recognized are these:

1. recognizing people during normal company events or other occasions;

2. making use of company newsletters, magazines, and other communication tools;

3. sending personal letters signed by a member of top management thanking people for contributions to the organization;

4. giving visible tokens of appreciation (books, caps, key chains, and so on).

- *Rewards* are extrinsic motivators that can have different meanings for people. Money can mean survival for people at the bottom of the pyramid and a winning score for people at the top. People are resentful when they feel they are not fairly paid, but as we have discussed, money does not usually engage the intrinsic motivation of knowledge workers.

There are exceptions. When I visited a Toyota assembly plant in Nagoya, I learned that workers were rewarded for creating harmony and helping others. In this way, Toyota not only reinforced collaboration, they were reinforcing the intrinsic motivation they sought in leaders.

- *Relationships*—people are motivated by good relationships with bosses, collaborators, partners and customers.

Of course, good relationships are not only motivating, but also essential for collaboration and partnering. The more people understand each other's personalities, the better able they are to work together and avoid destructive conflict. Soft motivational theories focus on caring leadership, but caring can become indulgent without knowledge of personality.

Relationships with customers, helping them solve problems, is motivating for caring people and also for interactives, who enjoy the interaction and chance to create value. When I was working at AT&T, I visited a business service center where I met a young woman I'll call Penny, a service technician and union member. Penny controlled a multi-million-dollar account with a business customer who only wanted to deal with her, not with her manager or the account executive. I asked her whether she could handle the responsibilities of serving this corporate customer. She said she was better with customer needs related to voice than data, but that her friend, Annie, helped her with data. I asked whether she had any use for a manager. "Of course," she answered. "I need him to tell me about new products and pricing." Clearly, management's role was not motivating Penny either with hard or soft motivations. Penny, a person with an interactive-adaptive personality, was motivated by her responsibilities and her relationships with the customer and her co-worker.

Marshall Goldsmith, the super-executive coach, lists habits a leader needs for good relationships, such as asking questions, listening carefully, responding to questions, and thanking collaborators. He has developed an exercise that shows how relationships between people at work can be improved. Relationships between bosses and subordinates are often strained by performance evaluation sessions, a form of feedback. We do appreciate immediate feedback when we perform an assigned task, and recognition is a positive form of feedback. However, people don't like to get negative evaluations and bosses don't like to give them. Marshall suggests an exercise he calls feedforward[9] to replace some kinds of feedback.

Feedforward can be a positive version of evaluative feedback. An example of the difference between feedback and feedforward might be a boss talking to a subordinate who has just given a bad presentation to an important customer. The subordinate knows he's screwed up. He doesn't need evaluative feedback. But he could use advice about improving his presentations in the future. That would be feedforward.

In the feedforward exercise, participants pick one behavior they would like to change. It could be listening better, planning activities better, avoiding conflicts, or any other behavior change that would make a significant, positive difference in their lives.

Participants randomly select partners. One person describes the behavior simply, such as "I want to be a better listener." The other person gives one or two suggestions for improvement. Participants are not allowed to comment on the suggestions or even say "That's a good idea." They should just say "Thanks." And the other person should say "You're welcome." Then the other participant is asked what s/he would like to change, and the process of giving and receiving feedforward is repeated. It usually lasts no more than two minutes for each person's feedforward. Participants should then find another partner and repeat the exercise.

Goldsmith has observed more than 10,000 leaders as they participated in feedforward. I participated in one directed by him and have observed hundreds in workshops I've led. When the exercise is finished, we've asked participants for one word that best describes the experience. The words have been almost always extremely positive, such as "great," "energizing," "useful," "helpful," "enjoyable," and even "fun."

I've asked participants why feedforward is so much better than feedback. Participants say it's not only more helpful, it's reciprocal. There is no hierarchy.

The Leadership Relationship

When I began to work as a consultant to IBM and AT&T in the late 1970s, good relationships between bosses and subordinates based on respectful paternalism were extremely motivating for people with a bureaucratic social character. Respect is still essential in all relationships at work, but interactive people are not looking for paternal figures to take care of them. They want to be treated as collaborators whose talents, views, and desire for learning are respected.

There is a difference between being motivated to do a job and being motivated to follow a leader. Some people are motivated by their work but turned off by their boss. When people leave organizations, a common reason is that they want to leave their boss. Interactives, especially, do not want to work with autocratic bosses.

Leadership is a relationship, and there are different reasons why people have been motivated to follow leaders. Effective leaders of change create the conditions that stimulate followers to become enthusiastic collaborators. They communicate a purpose that is meaningful to different types of personalities. They articulate and practice a philosophy for furthering a common purpose. They are also principled pragmatists; they are flexible in achieving their aims and able to use moral reasoning to make difficult ethical decisions between two "rights" or two "wrongs." They engage resistance with convincing logic.

To lead system change, leaders need to create understanding about the need for change and how a changed system will improve results. Leaders should develop a communication plan to explain why what worked in the past no longer does so, how the challenges of the present and future will be addressed by the idealized vision of the system. Only when collaborators understand the reasons for change will they be able to participate and contribute to the change process.

To carry out a vision of change, leaders must be able to motivate an organization, to create optimism and enthusiasm. Some people will be ready to collaborate from the start. Others may resist and will need to be persuaded that it's in their interest to follow. When a vision of change is presented, the first thoughts of people are "How will this affect me?," "What new things will I have to do?," "What things that I currently value will be lost?" Leaders should encourage people to think about taking on responsibilities that use and develop their strengths.

Motivating people to change in the face of adversity, challenging them to leave their comfort zone, is different from getting them to follow in less turbulent times. Many followers, especially those with a bureaucratic social character, want security, comfort, and a "one-minute manager," who gives them a measurable objective, leaves them alone, and later gives them a one-minute evaluation. Some, with a strong drive for power, feel their fiefdoms are threatened by change.

If we consider the motivations of both leaders and the led, we can describe four types of relationship. Leaders may be motivated to improve the common good or to gain personal power. Although motives may be mixed, leaders driven to gain power over others generally mask their motives in visions of the common good, but events reveal which motive is dominant. George Washington and Napoleon Bonaparte both claimed to work for the common good. But Washington returned to his farm at the end of his presidential terms while Napoleon made himself emperor and devastated France with his greed for conquest and power. People either *want to* follow leaders because some combination of their intrinsic and extrinsic motives is engaged, or they *have to follow* out of fear or need.

Table 7.1 describes these motives of leaders and led that produce four types of relationship.

Table 7.1. Motivations of leaders and led

		Motivation of led	
		Have to follow	Want to follow
Motivation of leader	Common good	Benevolent dictator	
		Doctor persuades	Democrat collaborates
	Personal power	Dictator dominates	Demagogue seduces

The Demagogue—People Want to Follow a Power-driven Leader

People who want to follow a leader who is out to gain personal power get a seductive demagogue like Napoleon who promised a progressive vision for France. Hitler promised the German people prosperity and glory, but when faced with defeat, ordered Albert Speer to destroy the country to punish Germany for failing him. In a less drastic way, people are taken in by leaders like Bernie Madoff or the leaders of Enron, who seduce them with dreams of wealth and glory, but deliver nightmares.

The Dictator—People Feel They Have to Follow a Power-driven Leader

People feel they have to follow a power-driven dictator out of fear. Leaders like Stalin and Saddam Hussein terrorize their followers. But on a smaller scale, these dictators may be sadistic bosses or teachers. Who among us has not had to suffer a dictator at school or work?

The Doctor—People Don't Want to Follow a Leader Working for the Common Good

When a leader of change, working for the common good, faces unmotivated or resistant people, there are different ways of dealing with these people. One way is to be a benevolent dictator who forces change with hard motivation, positive and negative incentives, rewarding those who change and threatening to fire those who won't budge. If the benevolent dictator produces great results, resisters may become willing followers. In contexts such as traditional Chinese culture, this type of leader may be especially effective, like Lee Kuan Yew, who attacked graft and corruption and bullied and built Singapore into a rich city-state.

But in the context of knowledge work and the interactive social character, the leader with resistant employees is more likely to gain willing followers by being the kind of doctor who uses the Five Rs to engage employees and persuade them to support change. Like the doctor who makes it clear that unless a patient with diabetes follows a new diet and exercises, he may end up in an emergency room, the leader should explain fully the reasons for change, answer all questions, and respond to all doubts. But if the patient refuses to change, the leader, like the doctor, will end the relationship.

Both a good doctor and a good leader want to make patient-followers into collaborators. When patients collaborate in managing their own chronic condition, they are more likely to stay healthy. When followers collaborate in the implementation of the vision, change is more likely to succeed.

People resist collaborating for different reasons. If doctor-leaders understand these reasons, they will be better able to treat resistance. The following are reasons for resistance to change:

1. Employees don't understand the vision and what it will mean for them and their roles.

When Jack Fearnsides was in charge of MITRE's Center for Advanced Aviation System Development (CAASD), he asked me to help him to implement

124

his vision of transforming traffic management of the air traffic control system to capacity management. He introduced me to a meeting of his subordinates and I asked what they thought of Jack's vision. "What vision?" one person asked. Jack repeated it. There was a long silence before another person asked whether he should stop working on his current project.

Jack's vision was complex. It required collaboration with the airlines as well as the Federal Aviation Administration (FAA). To increase air traffic capacity, airlines had to change their schedules and air traffic controllers needed training. Jack's team was used to technical work, and the vision called for people with interpersonal skills. To overcome resistance, Jack had to explain the purpose of change, clarify roles and responsibilities, and train his team.

2. Employees fear a loss of authority and clarity with change that makes them share authority. They may believe that change will be chaotic and unproductive. Robert Kagan and Lisa Laskow Lahey in their book *Immunity to Change*[10] describe effective ways of helping managers to become aware of and overcome egocentric mindsets that block change, such as pride in not having to rely or depend on others or belief that if they lose control things will go to hell.

In contrast, during the process of change at the Harman factory in Bolivar, Tennessee, Paul Reeves, a supervisor, taught his team members to take on part of his managerial role of planning, scheduling, quality control, evaluation, etc. When a company vice president suggested that Reeves might lose his authority, he answered, "Since I started giving it away, I never had so much authority." Formerly compliant workers were finding purpose in their own development and had become willing collaborators.

3. Good relationships can motivate negatively as well as positively. Employees who have formed tight cliques reject outsiders. Clearly, if leaders are unable to persuade members of a clique to get with the change program, they will have to break up the group.

4. The most difficult resisters to deal with are the ones who publicly comply with change, but privately scheme to undermine it. Leaders need to be ruthless about exposing compliers and firing them. They should clearly explain the reasons why they have made this decision.

5. Change requires healthy dialogue and debate. People will resist if debate based on facts and testable theories degenerates into personal conflict. In *Have a Nice Conflict*, Tim Scudder and associates provide good advice about avoiding conflict, aided by understanding personality.[11]

To persuade resisters to change, one has to connect with their values. It's also important not to devalue their past work. After the break-up of the Bell System, when part of the Bell Labs was being split off to become Bellcore, the R&D arm of the telephone operating companies, I was asked to lead workshops with groups of engineers and technicians aimed at changing their mindsets from monopoly to competitive thinking.

I gave the participants questionnaires that showed them having the social character of bureaucratic experts. I decided to appeal to their reason and professionalism, their values of survival and mastery. In the first two workshops, I described their social character and tried to persuade them that they had to change. Unless they became more responsive to their customers' demands, they were in danger of losing their business.

The result was that the participants gave me very low evaluations. I told my wife, a teacher, what happened. "I'm not surprised," she said. "You are talking to people who consider themselves members of the greatest R&D organization in the world. They invented lasers, touch phones and information technology. You are making them feel bad. To engage them, you must affirm their achievements."

I followed her advice and began the workshops by reviewing the great inventions and discoveries at the Bell Labs. Then I described the changing market environment and invited them to think about how they might change to compete and succeed. From then on, my evaluations were uniformly high.

The Democrat—People Want to Follow a Leader Working for the Common Good

A leader can be democratic with followers-collaborators when they share a purpose and practice the same values. It makes no sense to invite participation in decisions from people who don't share the organizational philosophy. But leaders who are trusted gain engaged and motivated collaborators by articulating, communicating, and practicing a philosophy that is inspiring, with goals that further the common good. When people freely collaborate with the fullest of energy, they become engaged. They accept empowerment and accountability.

Leading with Head and Heart

Reasons, responsibilities, recognition, and rewards are conceptual tools for leading change. To use them well, leaders need to understand the intrinsic motivation of the people they lead. But when leaders strengthen their hearts, they will greatly improve their ability to establish trust and develop motivating relationships.

Awareness of personality dynamics equips a leader to predict behavior and is a significant aid in selecting partners. However, as noted in Chapter 6, recognizing these patterns does not equip a leader to sense emotions such as fear, anxiety, doubt, resentment, and anger. By sensing and responding to emotions, leaders can turn fear into hope, doubt into determination. If leaders sense that followers feel debilitating anxiety, they can dissolve it by focusing energies on implementing a promising vision. If they do not paper over anger or resentment, they can explore and deal with the causes of these destructive emotions.

This ability is often termed emotional intelligence, but I believe it is better understood as a heart that listens. Emotional intelligence is about self-control and empathy, but a leader with personality intelligence understands the emotions that people experience in the context of the values that drive their behavior. This is the basis for emotional competency, the ability to sense negative emotions and then stimulate positive feelings. It employs both head and heart.

To develop your heart, recognize that both figuratively, as well as literally, the heart is a muscle. Without exercise, it won't get strong. Overly protected, it is easily hurt. There's a term for a person with a weak heart and a strong sense of guilt—*a bleeding heart*, typically someone who doesn't understand others but wants to help the underdog. When the object of these good intentions isn't grateful, the person feels taken in. His heart bleeds with disappointment and self-pity.

To avoid feeling vulnerable or being misled by their emotions, some managers build a shell around their hearts. One such CEO told me, "If I opened myself up to people, they would eat me alive." Another said, "I've a shell around my heart, and even my children feel and resent it." But their overprotected hearts cramped their effectiveness. It made these two executives vulnerable to subordinates who flattered them. This self-protectiveness leaves the unexercised heart flabby and causes leaders to obsess over decisions about people when they need to be decisive. The exercised heart becomes stronger through experiencing and understanding the feelings and values of other people.

Although they may have radar-like interpersonal intelligence, based on sharp awareness of language and facial expressions, leaders who are detached tend to use their gut rather than their hearts in deciding about people. This causes them to value people too much on appearance, on whether or not they look good, present themselves well, or seem confident. This is how George W. Bush made decisions about people, as when he boasted of understanding Vladimir Putin. Underneath these quick judgments often lurks unresolved doubt.

Of course, some leaders don't just protect a tender heart, but harden their hearts in the pursuit of power, revenge, or an ideology that justifies terrorism. These are the most dangerous leaders, who rule by fear and are not moved by others' feelings, like Fidel Castro, who was remorseless and unforgiving of his perceived enemies and wrote from prison, "I have a heart of steel."[12]

Developing the heart means exercising it, not detaching ourselves from strong and painful feelings. It means that leaders should not ignore the guilt they may feel when making an unpopular decision, firing people, or otherwise causing grief in order to further the common good, and not ignore the anger of those who are hurt. No muscle gets strengthened without painful exercise.

Just as there are disciplines to develop the intellect, such as mathematics, logic, and scientific methods, there are disciplines to develop the heart. They are: clearing the mind to see things as they are; listening to ourselves; and listening and responding to others with realism and compassion.

Disciplines of the Heart

> *One sees clearly only with the heart.*
>
> —Antoine De Saint-Exupéry

Clearing the mind means seeing things as they are, frustrating the cravings that cloud the mind, avoiding fantasy and all forms of escapism. Heraclitus wrote that when we dream, we are all in different worlds, but awake, we are in the same reality. Only when we are fully awake do we see things as they are, and many people go through life half-asleep because they repress uncomfortable perceptions and feelings.

To see things as they are, first of all, we have to frustrate the fantasies and passions that keep us from being clear-eyed and fully awake. But we can't frustrate irrational passions if we repress them. At an early age, we naturally repress thoughts and impulses that make us feel crazy or could get us into trouble. But the habit of repression can spread, blocking self-awareness.

There are different exercises to clear the mind or develop mindfulness, or *smrti*, a term that in Sanskrit is also translated as awareness. I have practiced the Zen Buddhist technique of meditation that includes breathing exercises as well as clearing the mind and becoming calmly aware of one's body and feelings. This exercise strengthens the ability to clear the mind. Other techniques are similar and lead to the same result.

Listening to ourselves requires experiencing what we would feel and think if we weren't defending ourselves from these unpleasant feelings and thoughts. We all have within us the human potentialities and passions, creative and destructive. An essential function of religious and philosophical thinking is to contain and give meaning to what we can experience when we become aware of powerful and troubling repressed feelings.

Although there's a limit to how much we can simultaneously function in the rough-and-tumble world and explore the depths of our psyches, we can practice getting in touch with what we really experience with other people and not repress uncomfortable thoughts and feelings. Of course, sometimes it's inconvenient to admit what we really feel about people we need to get along with. But we can't do anything about improving bad relationships if we don't see people as they are.

There are forms of meditation and prayer in different religious and philosophical traditions that help to connect us to our feelings and silence the noise that muffles the small voice of truth that is in all of us, but often is ignored. Also, by paying attention to our dreams, we sometimes become aware of perceptions of ourselves and of others that we've repressed because it would be uncomfortable to recognize them.[13]

If we have developed our personal philosophy, we are better able to deal with the challenging messages we are trying to give to ourselves. We become aware of the choices we may have to make between immediate pleasure and long-term happiness.

Listening and responding to others, once we have cleared the mind and are awake, frees us from the obsession with self. This kind of listening is active, reaching out with head and heart to understand what we are hearing. Paradoxically, obsessing about what others think of us feeds egocentrism. That just keeps us in ourselves. We only overcome egocentrism when we get out of ourselves to see things from another's point of view—which doesn't mean assuming that others feel what we'd feel in their place. Rather, we need to make an effort to understand how others view things through their own lenses, even experiencing directly what they experience, which is an effort of both head and heart. Beyond understanding is courageous service, reaching out to others, responding with intelligence and compassion.

Not only do we strengthen our ability to understand and act by practicing these disciplines, but also, as Albert Schweitzer wrote, only those who have sought and found how to serve well will be truly happy. By realizing a vocation of service, we strengthen our hearts and also attract others who share our goals.

Finally, a fully developed heart is a courageous heart. People will only fully trust leaders who demonstrate courage. Such leaders make a huge difference. They communicate a sense of the possible, a sense that together we can overcome our doubts and fears to achieve our vision.

Questions for Individuals on Smart Motivation

To develop the ability to create the conditions that will improve engagement and motivation of collaborators, consider how the Five Rs either motivate or demotivate you. Start with rank ordering of the Five Rs in terms of importance for your motivation using Table 7.2.

Table 7.2. What motivates you?

	Rank order	What motivates?	What demotivates?
Responsibilities			
Reasons			
Recognition			
Rewards			
Relationships			

Questions for Leaders on Smart Motivation

1. How do you communicate a purpose, a reason for being that is meaningful to your collaborators?

2. How do you place people in roles that connect with their values and skills?

3. How do you place people in jobs where they are challenged and are able to grow?

4. How do you try to drive out fear from the organization so that people are not afraid to be open and mistakes can be opportunities for learning?

5. How do you encourage healthy conflict and avoid conflict that causes resentment?

6. How do you recognize contributions to the organization?

7. Do people in your organization feel fairly rewarded?

8. How do rewards reinforce collaboration?

9. What are you doing to develop head and heart?

Notes

1. Michael Hammer and Steven Stanton, *The Re-engineering Revolution: The Handbook* (London: Harper Collins, 1995), pp. 30, 52.
2. H. F. Harlow, "Mice, Men, and Motives," *Psychological Review*, 60 (1953): 23–32.
3. See Edward L. Deci with Richard Flaste, *Why We Do What We Do: Understanding Self-motivation* (New York: Penguin Books, 1995).
4. Caring bosses who help employees with their personal and work problems shouldn't expect gratitude, loyalty, and commitment in return according to a study by IMD business school. Most managers believe offering emotional support will benefit their company, yet most employees simply view such shows of kindness as part of their superiors' duties and have no intention of working any harder by way of saying thank-you. "Workers Take Caring Bosses for Granted, Says IMD Study," 18 July 2013, at: <http://www.imd.org/news/Caring-Bosses.cfm> (accessed November 2014).

5. Peter Drucker, *The Practice of Management* (New York: Harper and Brothers, 1954). I observed the downside of MBO at AT&T when, to reach their cost objective, a division manager withheld products, causing the manager of another department to miss his sales objectives. While the first manager got a bonus, the company was the loser.

6. "Daniel Pink on Motivation," *The Washington Post* (9 January 2011), p. G02.

7. "Women in World War II," at: <http://www.nebraskastudies.org/0800/stories/0801_0135.html> (accessed November 2014).

8. Recent surveys of more than 12,000 mostly white-collar employees across a broad range of companies and industries, a manufacturing company with 6,000 employees, and a financial services company with 2,500 employees support the use of the Five Rs. The survey results were that employees were more satisfied and engaged when they felt valued and appreciated for their contributions (relationships and recognition); were doing more of what they do best and enjoy most (responsibilities); and felt connected to a higher purpose at work (reasons).
   Tony Schwartz and Christine Porath, "Why You Hate Work?," *New York Times* (1 June 2014).

9. Goldsmith's full description can be found at: <http://www.marshallgoldsmith.com> (accessed November 2014).

10. Boston, MA: Harvard Business School Press, 2009.

11. Tim Scudder, Michael Patterson, and Kent Mitchell, *Have a Nice Conflict* (San Francisco, CA: Jossey Bass, 2012).

12. Ann Louise Bardach, "Letters from Prison: Castro Revealed," *Washington Post*, (25 February 2007), Outlook, 5.

13. In his book, *The Forgotten Language*, Erich Fromm shows that dreams are often messages we are trying to tell ourselves (New York: Rinehart, 1951).

8

Dialogues with Deming

Without theory, experience has no meaning. Without theory, one has no questions to ask. Hence without theory, there is no learning . . . To copy an example of success without understanding it with the aid of theory may lead to disaster.

—W. Edwards Deming,
The New Economics

Both Russ Ackoff and W. Edwards Deming inspired me to develop conceptual tools for organizational transformation (see Figure 8.1). Both of these visionary thinkers invited me to join them in stimulating dialogues that sharpened my thinking.

This chapter describes:

- learnings from Deming;
- comparisons of Ackoff and Deming and their contributions to the concept of strategic intelligence;
- responses to Deming's question of whether national character determines organizational culture.

Meeting Deming

In 1989, Clare Crawford-Mason came to my office with an invitation to meet Deming. He had liked my book, *Why Work*[1] and wanted to talk with me about motivation and leadership. Deming had become famous as the father of the Japanese quality revolution because of an NBC documentary, *If Japan Can, Why Can't We*, that aired in June 1980. Because of the documentary, American companies hired Deming as a quality consultant and he packed workshops with managers and consultants eager to learn his methods. Clare produced the documentary and went on to produce the Deming Library, videotapes of

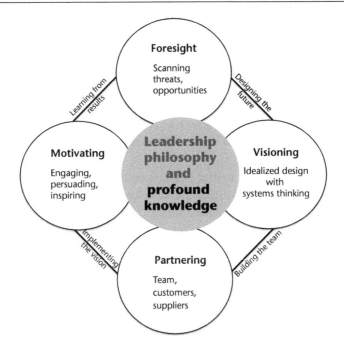

Figure 8.1. Strategic intelligence—highlighting Deming's concept of profound knowledge

Deming expounding his theories and participating in dialogues with others who complemented his thinking.

For more than three years I met periodically with Deming, sharing ideas and making videotapes with him on motivation and leadership. Clare also transcribed a lengthy discussion we had about leadership and culture change. I was flattered and inspired that Deming, in his 90s, was taking notes of what I was saying. He was still learning, and you can see in his books that he cites a number of people who were sources of his learning.

What Deming Achieved

In an extensively researched essay, including interviews with key Japanese management experts, William M. Tsutsui described Deming's work in Japan and concluded that his achievements were greatly exaggerated.[2]

He writes that Deming "was a facilitator, not a creator, a prodigy of public relations rather than a genius of management strategy."[3] Tsutsui writes that the Japanese understood quality before Deming arrived, and developed management practices that went beyond Deming's teachings about statistics and quality. Deming acknowledged Japanese knowledge of quality. He wrote, "...the quality of Japanese consumer goods had earned around the world

133

a reputation for being shoddy and cheap. Yet anyone in our Navy will testify that the Japanese knew what quality is. They simply had not yet bent their efforts toward quality in international trade."[4]

However, Tsutsui quotes Japanese quality experts who honored Deming as a friend of Japan, who "made us believe that there would be a possibility to improve quality even amidst the disaster of the Second World War."[5]

When I asked Deming whether he had taught the Japanese quality management, he said, "It wasn't that. I made them believe they could be the best in the world."

What Tsutsui leaves out is that Deming learned from the Japanese. From his intellectual base in statistics, he developed theories of management, influenced in large part by Japanese practice and culture. When I met him, he had published his concepts of profound knowledge and the fourteen points that summarized his philosophy of organizational transformation.[6] Deming also inspired disciples, who went on to develop techniques to apply his theories.[7]

Deming's Ideal of Transformation

I asked Deming whether any of the American companies he had advised during the past ten years had transformed themselves. His answer was a firm "No!" A number of companies had adopted parts of his approach, especially statistical process control. There was a burgeoning business of quality consultants and training to gain black belts, especially in the auto industry that had been humbled by the quality of Japanese cars. But for Deming, this was not transformation. Transformation required systemic culture change, not only improved processes, but leadership that practiced Deming's philosophy. He said he had learned much by observing the best-run Japanese companies. However, he tailored his learning for Western management. In his book, *Out of the Crisis*, he introduced the fourteen points of his philosophy in a chapter entitled "Principles for Transformation of Western Management."[8]

Box 8.1 JAPANESE QUALITY: AN INSTRUCTIVE FABLE?

When I was giving leadership workshops to Ford managers in 1991, a plant manager related how he first encountered Japanese quality. He had contracted Honda as a supplier with the proviso that there would be only 2 percent quality rejects of the products Honda supplied. When the first one hundred products arrived, there were two packages wrapped separately from the other ninety-eight. He asked the Honda representative what was in the two packages. The answer: "Those are the two rejects you asked for." I later learned that this story was also told about IBM and Texas Instruments. It had become folklore.

This is what I took from dialogues with Deming.

- Deming emphasized the importance of leadership to create constancy of purpose toward improvement of products and services and to lead change. He encouraged me to continue to develop the concepts on leadership and philosophy presented in Chapters 3 and 4. However, Deming described only one type of leadership, which essentially combined strategic and operational leadership with a Confucian model that emphasizes mentoring.

- Deming showed that by building quality into the work process, not only will quality improve but costs will also go down and productivity will be improved. Deming asked rhetorically, "Why is it that productivity increases as quality improves? Less rework. There is no better answer." As quality improves, there will be less need for inspection and less rework, as processes are better designed. Cliff and Jane Norman have put this theory to work in healthcare organizations and we describe these practices in our book, *Transforming Health Care Leadership, A Systems Guide to Improve Patient Care, Decrease Cost, and Improve Population Health.*[9] In a sense, I have continued learning from Deming by working with his disciples.

- Deming stated that by "driving out fear" from the workplace, everyone will work more effectively. They will be more likely to offer ideas and ask good questions. He showed that most errors attributed to workers are the result of faulty processes, not worker mistakes. When workers are blamed for system errors, they are afraid to report what happened. They hide errors, and there is no learning.

Box 8.2 DRIVING OUT FEAR AT AT&T

At AT&T, technicians sometimes cut the long-distance cables by mistake, resulting in the loss of many calls. Because they were afraid of punishment, they didn't report their mistakes. As a result, there was no learning about how to avoid these mistakes or quickly correct them. A new head of the long-distance network instituted a policy of no punishment for reporting mistakes and organized a team that designed a process for avoiding cable cuts.

Deming's focus on reducing common cause variation in a system that causes errors while engaging all employees in continuous improvement proved good advice for driving out fear and stimulating learning. However, when I asked groups of managers to indicate the amount of fear in their organization versus what it should be on a scale of one (no fear) to four (extreme fear), almost all of them indicated that while the current number was three or four, it should be two, not one. They believed people needed some fear to motivate them, otherwise they might get too comfortable. But the fear should be focused on the competition, not the boss. When I reported this to Deming, his comment was "Interesting."

- Deming urged managers to break down barriers between departments. This was consistent with a systems view of the organization. It is also essential for concurrent engineering where design, engineering, production, and marketing work together to cut the costs and time needed to produce a product. However, I have found that this requires network leaders, able to facilitate collaboration.

- Deming emphasized education and training on the job not only to improve technical competence but also understanding of systems, variation, psychology, and creating knowledge. He insisted that without theory there is no improvement, innovation, or learning. Building on the work of Walter A. Shewhart, he developed Shewhart's cycle for testing hypotheses. This ultimately became the PDSA (plan–do–study–act) cycle of planning to test a theory of how change will improve a process, doing the test, studying what was learned from the test, and acting to make the changes that will improve the process (see Figure 8.2). Once improvements are made, new ideas may be proposed and the cycle can be repeated. Those who use this method ask three questions:[10]

1 What are we trying to accomplish?
2 How will we know a change is an improvement?
3 What changes can we make that will result in improvement?

Using the PDSA cycle helps to avoid what Chris Argyris called single-loop learning.[11] This occurs when the results of our practice don't fit our theory and we interpret this as a need to change or fine-tune our practice. Double-loop learning occurs when we question theory as well as practice. Using the PDSA cycle doesn't guarantee double-loop learning—people have a strong tendency to hold on to their theories—but it can stimulate us to question theories that fail to predict expected results (see Figure 8.3).

- Deming advised ending the practice of awarding business on the basis of price. Instead, he counseled that companies should minimize total cost over time, moving toward a single supplier on a long-term relationship of loyalty and trust.[12] This counsel encouraged me to develop the partnering continuum shown in Chapter 2.

However, when a company depends solely on a single supplier for a key part, a supplier problem can interrupt the whole production process. Some companies that followed Deming's advice, like Ford, have had this problem

Figure 8.2. PDSA cycle

Adapted from Gerald J. Langley, Ronald D. Moen, Kevin M. Nolan, Thomas W. Nolan, Clifford I. Norman, and Lloyd P. Provost, *The Improvement Guide: A Practical Approach to Enhancing Organizational Performance,* 2nd edn (San Francisco, CA: Jossey-Bass, 2009).

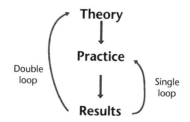

Figure 8.3. Single- and double-loop learning

Box 8.3 THEORIES VERSUS EVIDENCE

All too often, CEOs are surrounded by courtiers who flatter them and are afraid to challenge their theories, even when they have evidence to disprove them. A CEO who was proud of his program to engage employees was presented with survey findings that reported wide distrust of top management by the rest of the organization. He turned to his VPs and said, "This can't be true. I go around and talk with people all the time, and no one has told me this." The VPs who knew that no one dared to bring bad news to the CEO, all agreed that there must be something wrong with the survey or the way the questions were phrased.

---

and retreated to multiple suppliers. However, this does not contradict the principle of selecting suppliers according to total cost.

• Deming's views on managing and motivating employees were based on an idealized view of Japanese management. It was in some respects different from what I observed in Japan more then thirty years after Deming left.

Deming was right about some Japanese practices that were aimed at transforming bureaucracies into learning organizations. The best Japanese management does not employ Management by Objectives (MBO) that allows managers autonomy in reaching objectives. Instead, managers collaborate on developing and continuously improving processes.

Deming taught that all measurements of individual performance, all comparative ratings of workers, cause bad feelings and rivalries that undercut motivation and collaboration. He believed that leadership was responsible for the system. Leaders should design processes that facilitate quality work. Leaders are also responsible for training workers to do a good job. He argued that material incentives alone do not work. Good leaders engage intrinsic motivation and make work joyful.

However, I have pointed out in Chapter 7 that at Toyota, workers are measured and rewarded for demonstrating leadership skills such as teaching others and creating harmony. Toyota management also recognizes and rewards workers who offer ideas to improve productivity that are adopted. These rewards reinforce behavior that supports the Toyota values.

Deming and I agreed that productive motivation is gained by engaging intrinsic drives and that rewards can be demotivating. But I argued that rewards reinforcing organizational values such as leadership, collaboration, and continuous improvement, can strengthen individual engagement and organizational success. One result of the transformation process at MITRE was that employees were no longer measured and rewarded solely on technical competence but on a combination of qualities that also included leadership and customer responsiveness. This resulted in better relations with customers and colleagues. Deming agreed that reasons, responsibilities, and relationships engaged intrinsic motivation, but he remained skeptical of any kind of reward or recognition. He believed that creating the conditions for pride of workmanship is enough to engage workers. Furthermore, he had not thought about the role of different motivational value systems and their relationship to work roles and relationships. But when I described this, he took notes.

Deming vs Ackoff

Ackoff, Deming, and I noted that each of us had been influenced by American philosophers of pragmatism: Charles Pierce, William James, John Dewey, and

Clarence I. Lewis. James contrasted tough-minded thinkers, who believe nothing is true unless it can be measured, with tender-minded thinkers, who believe nothing is true unless it fits their values. Neither of these people, James argued, owned the truth. We all have beliefs, but the pragmatist tests them and is open to modifying them if they fail to predict or explain results. Both Ackoff and Deming taught that improvements are gained by testing theories and hypotheses, and Deming used versions of the PDSA cycle as a testing tool. I developed the process for constructing an organizational philosophy while reading James on pragmatism.[13] Although Ackoff and Deming shared a formation in the teachings of pragmatism and they agreed on the importance of system transformation, they had different visions of leadership and the process of change.

In 1992, I helped Clare Crawford-Mason bring Ackoff and Deming together to discuss organizational change (see Figure 8.4). Both agreed that change should be systemic. Both agreed that in transforming an organization, you should innovate and create, not copy others. Both wanted a system that produced products and services that improved the quality of life for customers and that stimulated the continual development of people as well as processes. But their visions of change clashed.

Ackoff's ideal was a democratic corporation where groups of employees and customers were empowered to initiate change.[14] The leader-architect had the task of integrating these bottom-up initiatives into a system that was efficient, effective, and aesthetically pleasing.

Figure 8.4. Photo of Maccoby, Ackoff, and Deming from 1992
Source: CC-M Productions.

For Deming, this was an upside-down view of transformation. His vision called for an expert leader to design a system with processes that assured quality and allowed employees to enjoy pride of workmanship. Everyone should participate in continuous improvement, but it should be led by managers with the knowledge essential to understand the system and its interactive processes. He considered most QC-Circles and Employee Involvement programs as "cruel hoaxes" that quickly run out of ideas or fail to accomplish anything because no one in management takes action on suggestions for improvement.[15] Unless people had the theory and knowledge to integrate ideas into a system, making changes would be destructive, tampering with the system.

However, Ackoff was advocating bottom-up change within a system. Sometimes, this may be the best way to initiate change. The top-down approach can become too rigid, as in the case of Florida Power and Light (FPL), a company that in 1989 won the Japanese Deming Prize for its quality program. FPL set up a business to teach its methods to other companies, but its service costs began rising and a few years later a new CEO disbanded the program and closed the teaching company. What happened was that the service technicians had been handed exact instructions to follow processes to fix electrical outages. But in Florida, problems varied in different areas and called for different solutions. Based on their experiences, the technicians had filled notebooks with guidelines and processes to deal with problems in city high rises, rural areas with thick vegetation, suburbs, beach fronts, and so on. When told to follow the quality instructions, they left their notebooks in their lockers, and the result was less efficient, more costly work.

Deming's approach to an ideal design fit well for manufacturing and services with repetitive tasks. Both his and Ackoff's approaches can be effective. It depends on the context.

Innovation

Deming pointed out that a company could reduce defects to zero and still go out of business. Ackoff agreed that both product and process innovation were essential for a company to succeed. But they disagreed about what creates innovation. Ackoff believed that by competing for the satisfaction of customers and responding to their needs, competition can produce innovation.

Deming strongly disagreed. He said, "Customers don't generate anything. They want only what you and your competitors have led them to expect. No customer asked for electric lights. No customer asked for photography. No customer asked for a telegraph. No customer asked for a telephone nor an automobile, nor for pneumatic tires, nor for integrated circuits." He went on to say that producers should look ahead of customers to satisfy a social *need* such as transportation and communication, in new and better ways.

Deming pointed to innovators at the Bell Labs, who like professors with tenure, were free to develop inventions like fax machines, transistors, lasers, solar batteries, and mobile telephones. But there was also evidence to support Ackoff's view. AT&T refused to digitize the phone system until competitors forced them to do so. They gave away the invention of mobile telephony and had to buy it back from a competitor. Invention is not innovation until it is put to work, and the Bell Labs held on to inventions until others applied them and made them innovations.

Furthermore, monopolies can oppress customers and suppliers. After the break-up of the Bell System, I was hired by the IT division of Bellcore, that part of the Bell labs that was assigned to the operating telephone companies, to interview their operating company customers about how they felt about their relationship with the Bell Labs. Engineers in the various telephone companies that had been part of the Bell System said they resented the arrogant Bell Labs engineers. They had been forced to follow their directions. Now, they were happy to be free of the Bell Labs and to be able to compete against them.

Both Ackoff and Deming could point to examples that supported their views. Competition can be healthy as long as there are rules of the game that protect the players and customers from theft, fraud, and collusion of companies. But competition does not guarantee innovation or progress. It was not competition that motivated leaders like William Mayo to create the best healthcare organizations. In one case, competition undermined a promising cooperative initiative in Rochester, New York. The hospitals got together and decided to collaborate rather than compete. Each hospital would have a different specialty so all of them would not need to invest in the same expensive technology. This could improve competence, as each hospital would have increased experience in its specialty, and lower costs. The plan was torpedoed by the CEO of Kodak, the largest company in Rochester and biggest customer of health care. He maintained that without competition, there would be no innovation or progress. Each hospital then invested in all the technologies; costs increased without any evidence of improved results.

Both competition and freedom contribute to innovation. Both are important, just as both the political competition of democracy and the protections of individual liberty are both essential to a free society.

Contributions to Strategic Intelligence

Strategic intelligence integrates concepts I learned from Ackoff, Deming, and Fromm, together with those I have developed myself. I learned different aspects of systems thinking from all three. From Ackoff, I learned about organizational visions as social systems, idealized design, and backward interactive planning to move toward the vision. From Deming, I learned about designing and continually improving a system of processes. I also learned about variation, understanding the difference between special and common causes, and avoiding the attribution error of blaming a worker for errors caused by faulty processes. From Fromm, who was also a systems thinker, I learned about social character and it variations.

My contributions were to develop the strategic intelligence model, including leadership and organizational philosophy, personality intelligence, the Five Rs of motivation, and the partnering continuum. Although Ackoff and Deming had different views of leadership, both supported my concept of strategic, operational, and network leaders working interactively. Figure 8.5 describes the contributions and learning that contributed to strategic intelligence.

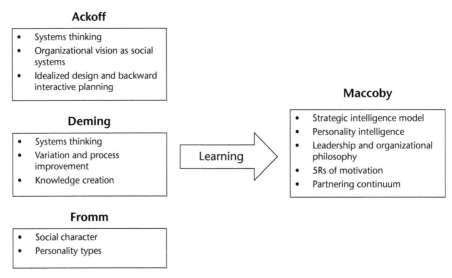

Figure 8.5. Contributions to strategic intelligence

The Conceptual Toolkit

The conceptual tools presented in this book should be viewed systemically. Their purpose is to develop qualities of mind and heart that equip leaders for strategic change. The concepts are best understood as they interact.

Foresight is strengthened by *partnering* to gain observations through different lenses and by a *leadership philosophy*, which, by articulating the organization's purpose and values, focuses scanning on trends most likely to affect the organization.

The Five Ps—purpose, products, people, processes, and practical values—aid *visioning*. People and processes can be understood by using the four concepts of *profound knowledge*: *systems thinking, variation, psychology* (personality intelligence), and *creating knowledge*. Leadership philosophy includes purpose and practical values.

Partnering and *motivating* employ personality intelligence, which, conceptually, is based on the patterns of social character and its variations as personality types. Good partners share the organization's philosophy. Personality, including social character and personality types, are formed from the seven value drives. The Five Rs of motivation connect personality to the social system formed from the Five Ps. The intrinsic motivation of people is engaged when their values connect to the organization's purpose and to their responsibilities (processes).

I have packaged these conceptual tools to be more easily remembered (see Figure 8.6). As with many tools, they are used more effectively with practice.

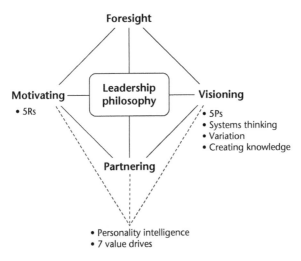

Figure 8.6. The conceptual toolkit

Culture Change and National Character

For Deming, transformation meant culture change from competitive Western industrial bureaucracies to an idealized vision of the organization as a cooperative system with a purpose. Despite his efforts, he did not think any of the American companies he had advised had changed their culture.

He asked if I thought that individualistic, competitive Americans could create the kind of cooperative companies he saw in Japan. I said that although it may be easier to create cooperative organizations in Japan, Toyota showed that they could be developed in the US when it transformed a GM factory.

NUMMI (New United Motor Manufacturing, Inc.) was a joint venture of GM with Toyota established in 1984 in Fremont, California. The NUMMI venture took over a GM plant that had been shut down because of worker unrest and low productivity. Despite inheriting a combative local union and workforce, Toyota's manager transformed the plant so that it was comparable in productivity and quality to Toyota's Japanese plants.

Toyota's ideology was expressed at NUMMI in many ways. While engineers at GM automated jobs in order to cut costs, NUMMI had robots that were designed to make people's jobs easier—for example, robots that do heavy lifting. The idea was that technology should be a tool and that workers should add wisdom to the machines with their ideas for improvement. Moreover, Toyota emphasized the exercise of leadership at every level to create trust and facilitate learning—a point that US manufacturers have neglected in focusing on how Toyota eliminates inventory, defects, and waste. At NUMMI, workers who taught and helped others were promoted to team leadership roles. Foremen are even given a budget to entertain workers periodically, buy them a beer, and strengthen relationships within teams.

In "Time and Motion Regained,"[16] Paul S. Adler, a sociologist who interviewed employees at NUMMI, wrote that workers were made to feel important; their views carried weight.

Although some NUMMI workers complained about the fast pace and about group pressure within teams, they still participated in ongoing learning and continuous improvement.

Is this emphasis on leadership particular to Japan? The managerial ideal in cultures based on Confucian thinking is, to some degree, the benevolent but demanding teacher/leader who creates strong bonds of mutual obligation. But not all Japanese companies are alike. Honda's approach emphasizes creative conflict, whereas Toyota's approach stresses benevolent hierarchy. Toyota's leadership ideology is rooted in a rural feudal culture and social character, whereas Honda's team ideology emerged in urban Tokyo. The Toyota worker was typically a farm boy in Nagoya, brought by his parents to the factory and handed over to management *in loco parentis*; by contrast, the typical Honda worker, with a more interactive social character, was a member of a motorcycle gang in Tokyo who brought a rough egalitarianism to a company that was itself rebelling against the Japanese establishment. (The government had disapproved of Honda's entering an already crowded market.) Company lore recounts how the engineer who stood up to and disagreed with founder Soichiro Honda eventually became president. In Toyota and Honda, we see different social characters in the same national culture.

Toyota, more than Honda, fits Deming's model. Whereas Toyota attacks problems with established teams and standardized methods, Honda boasts of spontaneous solutions. Everyone with relevant knowledge gets together to solve, say, a quality problem and then the group disbands. Honda breaks down boundaries between functions by requiring designers to spend time in production and engineers to sell cars. At the Honda plant in Marysville, Ohio, managers and engineers regularly work on the line for up to an hour each day. Honda's cross-functional teams that design new cars are not hierarchies but "heterarchies," in which leadership shifts according to who has the appropriate knowledge.

Toyota and Honda, in their unique ways, develop and align competencies, both technical and interpersonal, with the goals of quality production. In both cases, corporate philosophy reinforces the system. Few US companies (or, for that matter, few companies anywhere, including Japan) understand or are able to create such effective systems—systems that integrate and shape employees' values and competencies with a strong philosophy.[17]

Americans have a tradition of cooperating when there is a crisis or an enemy. At AT&T, employees ignored bureaucratic rules and roles when they had to restore service after a hurricane, fire, or flood. But when there is no crisis, Americans have valued autonomy above all else. The form of autonomy sought has changed together with changes in the mode of production and social character. For farmers, craftsmen, and owners of small businesses, autonomy means independence. For the bureaucratic personality, autonomy means having the freedom to decide the way of meeting objectives, something strongly opposed by Deming. For the interactive social character, autonomy means being a free agent, not tied to a role or an organization.

Whatever the social character, people in the US want to be their own boss. If they can't be, they want as much autonomy as possible. Americans may recognize they need leadership, but they would rather do the leading themselves. Immigrants to America have been attracted to this ideal.

A culture that values autonomy does not produce many leaders. Most business professionals in the US, both bureaucratic and interactive types, become managers not because they want to be leaders, but because management is a chore they are required to perform in order to be promoted. There are, of course, remarkable leaders and coaches who develop people, and create cooperation, but they are the exceptions and they command high salaries. Most Americans get ahead in business not because they are good leaders, but because they get results and get along with the boss.

For example, both Toyota and Honda have created effective cross-functional teams that use input to design cars for ease of production. Toyota does this with strong leadership and Honda with team competence. But when US automakers have tried to adopt these approaches, they have floundered, as managers of design or engineering have asserted their autonomy and defended their turf.

Yet as NUMMI demonstrated, US workers do respond to leaders who teach useful skills and business perspectives, communicate market and process information and reasons behind decisions, and facilitate problem-solving sessions. They respond to incentives based on collaboration. If they can't be autonomous, employees at least want a say in how their work is done. The workers I met in Scotland and Sweden may be less driven to gain autonomy, but just as happy to have a say in decisions that affect them. National character can make a difference, but it is trumped by social character and human nature.

The Culture of Learning Organizations

Both Ackoff and Deming complained that their ideas were only partially used by managers who hired them as consultants. Ackoff blamed managers for a lack of guts.[18] Deming blamed national character and a competitive mindset, with a focus on short-term profit. In fact, financial control differs between countries. The American and British finance systems are very rigorous and short- term oriented. When finance people ask every week or second week for financial information that few people understand, the result is financial game playing to meet targets and pressure on operations that can undermine strategic intelligence. In contrast, the Japanese typically have a longer time perspective on investments. Both Ackoff and Deming blamed business schools for this and for not teaching systems thinking and transformation.

The examples of Japanese management in the US as well as healthcare organizations such as the Mayo Clinic, Intermountain Health Care, IBM, and others my colleagues and I have worked with, prove that although it's more difficult for public companies facing short-term pressure, American companies can become innovative learning organizations. There is no standard culture of a learning organization. The culture will depend on the type of product and customer relationship on the partnering continuum. Even with similar products, the personal philosophy of the founder can influence the organizational culture as the contrast between Toyota and Honda demonstrates.

Any company can become a learning organization with its unique culture. But as Deming used to say, there is no instant pudding. It takes time, consistency of purpose, and it requires leaders with the conceptual tools of strategic intelligence. The Appendix presents exercises for developing strategic intelligence.

Notes

1. Michael Maccoby, *Why Work: Leading the New Generation* (New York: Simon & Schuster, 1988); Michael Maccoby, *Why Work? Motivating the New Work Force*, 2nd edn (Alexandria: Miles River Press, 1995).
2. William M. Tsutsui, "W. Edwards Deming and the Origins of Quality Control in Japan," *Journal of Japanese Studies*, Vol 22(2) (Summer, 1996): 295–325.
3. William M. Tsutsui, "W. Edwards Deming and the Origins of Quality Control in Japan," *Journal of Japanese Studies*, Vol 22(2) (Summer, 1996): 325.
4. W. Edwards Deming, *Out of the Crisis* (Cambridge, MA: MIT Press, 1982, 1986), p. 485.
5. William M. Tsutsui, "W. Edwards Deming and the Origins of Quality Control in Japan," *Journal of Japanese Studies*, Vol 22(2) (Summer, 1996): 313.
6. W. Edwards Deming, *Out of the Crisis* (Cambridge, MA: MIT Press, 1982, 1986); W. Edwards Deming, *The New Economics* (Cambridge, MA: MIT Press, 1994).
7. Gerald L. Langley, Ronald D. Moen, Kevin M. Nolan, Thomas W. Nolan, Clifford L. Norman, and Lloyd P. Provost, *The Improvement Guide. A Practical Approach to Enhancing Organizational Performances*, 2nd edn (San Francisco, CA: Jossey Bass, 2009).
8. W. Edwards Deming, *Out of the Crisis* (Cambridge, MA: MIT Press, 1982, 1986), p. 18.
9. Michael Maccoby, Clifford L. Norman, Jane Norman, and Richard Margolies, *Transforming Health Care Leadership: A Systems Guide to Improve Patient Care, Decrease Costs, and Improve Population Health* (San Francisco, CA: Jossey Bass, 2013).
10. Michael Maccoby, Clifford L. Norman, Jane Norman, and Richard Margolies. *Transforming Health Care Leadership: A Systems Guide to Improve Patient Care, Decrease Costs, and Improve Population Health* (San Francisco, CA: Jossey Bass, 2013), p. 179.
11. Chris Argyris, "Double Loop Learning in Organizations," *Harvard Business Review*, September–October (1977): 115–25.
12. Total cost = Price tag + Cost to use: Cost to use includes receiving inspection, supplier audits, scrap, rework, schedule problems related to the supplier.
13. William, James, *The Works of William James, Pragmatism* (Cambridge, MA: Harvard University Press, 1975).
14. Russell L Ackoff. *The Democratic Corporation, a Radical Prescription for Recreating Corporate America and Rediscovering Success* (New York: Oxford University Press, 1994).
15. There is evidence for Deming's view in the studies I reviewed in Michael Maccoby, "Is There a Best Way to Build a Car," *Harvard Business Review*, November–December (1997): 161–72.
16. Paul S. Adler, "Time and Motion Regained," *Harvard Business Review*, January–February 1993: 97–108.
17. I am grateful to John Paul MacDuffie for his observations on Toyota and Honda.
18. At a Ford executive workshop I attended that was led by Ackoff, an executive asked, "Russ, how many times have you given this workshop at Ford?" "About 50 times," said Ackoff. "And how many managers have implemented your ideas?" "None," said Ackoff." "Why not, Russ?" The answer, "No guts."

9

Building on the Work of Ackoff, Deming, and Fromm

Declaration of Interdependence[1]

We envision a new sector of the economy

which harnesses the power of private enterprise to create public benefit. This sector is comprised of a new type of corporation—the B Corporation—which is purpose-driven, and creates benefit for all stakeholders, not just shareholders.

As members of this emerging sector and as entrepreneurs and investors in B Corporations,

We hold these truths to be self-evident:

That we must be the change we seek in the world.

That all business ought to be conducted as if people and place mattered.

That, through their products, practices, and profits, businesses should aspire to do no harm and benefit all.

To do so, requires that we act with the understanding that we are each dependent upon another and thus responsible for each other and future generations.

—The B Corp Declaration

Great organizations are works of art, performing art. As with any art, the artists use science. For Ackoff, the creative organizational leader is an architect with aesthetic as well as technical qualities. Creative organizational leaders are also choreographers of a dance without end.

Just as there are relatively few great paintings, sculptures, and buildings, so there are relatively few great organizations. Just as it is difficult to define great art, so is it difficult to determine what makes an organization great. In his book, *Good to Great*,[2] Jim Collins defines great corporate organizations in terms of their share price, beating the market over time. This definition leads Collins to include companies that did well for a few years, but are no longer in business, and a tobacco company where the effect of its product on its customers is certainly not great. Collins does modify his formula by proposing that to maintain greatness, companies need an organizational philosophy with core values and a purpose other than profits. In this, he was inspired, as I was, by observing HP and interviewing its founders when they were still running the company.

In *The Living Company*,[3] Arie de Geus described the qualities of companies that have survived more than 100 years in terms that expand on Collins' view of lasting greatness. These qualities include adapting to change, learning, and developing people.

These qualities of survival are necessary attributes of great companies, as is profitability. But more is needed to define great organizations that are works of art. Leo Tolstoy defined art as " . . . a means of union among men, joining them together in the same feelings, and indispensible for the life and progress toward well-being of individuals and humanity." If we replace "men" with "men and women," Tolstoy's definition fits a description of great organizations that are works of art. Great organizations unite men and women, joining them together in the same feelings for the life and progress toward the well-being of individuals and humanity.

According to Deming, companies should produce products that better meet a human need such as transportation, energy, nutrition, and communication. According to Ackoff, products should improve the quality of life for customers. Fromm evaluates organizations in terms of whether or not they develop the social character. Do they encourage individuation, collaboration, and respect for life? Or do they demand conformity with group narcissism and exploit employees and the environment? Taken together, the views of these thinkers expand on the Tolstoyan definition of art applied to organizations.

Like great art, great organizations inspire and influence new ways of experiencing life. Building on the theories of Ackoff, Deming, and Fromm, great organizations can be defined by the following attributes:

- They are learning organizations with a purpose of improving their customers' quality of life and/or capability. If their customers are businesses, they help them to succeed. If they are healthcare organizations, their purpose is to improve patient care and increase population health in a way that is affordable. If they are homes for orphans and abandoned children, like NPH, their purpose is the care and development of the children as productive and caring citizens of their countries. If they are government organizations, their purpose may be national defense, administrating justice, protecting liberty, regulating and promoting commerce, and serving the public to improve health, education, and welfare, and to protect the natural environment. Great organizations constantly change, not only to adapt, but to innovate and improve.

- A product of work is the people who work in the organization. Great organizations develop people at work, not only their competence but also their character.

- Great organizations, like some of the companies described in Chapter 4 and the B Corporations, work to continually improve their social and environmental impact.

Unlike most other works of art, organizations, especially companies, are continually buffeted by change. Companies that aspire to be great in these terms sometimes have to balance their aspirations with the pressures of competition and impatient shareholders. Even though the values of conscious capitalism may pay off in the long run, they can add short-term costs. For example, *The Economist* reports that "Unilever aims to 'help a billion people to take steps to improve their health and well-being'; halve the environmental impact of its products, and source all its agricultural raw materials sustainably, meaning that they should meet requirements covering everything from forest production to pest control."[4] Unilever has made progress on energy use and waste production. But the Unilever share price has suffered. Although the company fails to achieve Collins' definition of great, it may prove to be greater in the long run than those that just hit an economic target.

The success of companies like Unilever, GE, and IBM, and healthcare organizations like Mayo and Intermountain in the US and Jönköping in Sweden[5] is important not only for their impact on customers, patients, workers, and communities. These organizations will be models for others, and they will be at the forefront of shaping the social character, the attitudes and values of the people who will control the most advanced mode of production in the future. If these organizations succeed, they will attract and develop the most talented people. There is evidence for this. A Brookings Institution study by Morley Wingrad and Michael Hais reports that almost all members of the Millenial Generation in the US (probably mostly interactives) responded with increased trust (91 percent) and loyalty (89 percent), as well as a stronger likelihood to buy from those companies that supported solutions to specific social issues (89 percent)."[6] The authors write that the "desire on the part of Millenials for their daily work to reflect and be a part of their societal concerns will make it impossible for corporate chieftains to motivate Millennial employees simply by extolling profits, or return on investment for their shareholders, or even their employee salaries."[7] It may well be that in the future, the most talented members of this generation will want to work for or build great companies with the attributes described here. If so, these companies will likely become the most successful in the long run. And shaping the social character needed for success in these companies will be the aim of education.

In the age of industrial bureaucracies, the most successful companies like Ford and AT&T were the organizational models for other companies and government. Schools trained people to fit bureaucratic roles. We are currently in a period of transition to a knowledge-service (technoservice) mode of production. We need great organizations to develop the most advanced knowledge to improve the lives of people on this planet. And we need leaders with qualities of mind and heart and the conceptual tools to make this happen. They will not develop these qualities by following formulas or narrowing their goals to satisfy shareholders. The qualities of strategic intelligence and profound knowledge require an interdisciplinary education that includes systems thinking in relation to economics, psychology, statistics, including the theory of variation, knowledge creation, cultural anthropology, history, and the humanities.

Leaders who aspire to create great organizations may not succeed. Few artists achieve greatness. But the changes they make that move an organization toward greatness will give meaning to work and improve our culture.

Notes

1. The B Corp Delaration, at: <http://www.bcorporation.net/what-are-b-corps/the-b-corp-declaration> (accessed November 2014).
2. Jim Collins, *Good to Great* (New York: Harper Business, 2001).
3. Arie de Geus, *The Living Company* (Boston, MA: Harvard Business School Press, 1997).
4. *The Economist* (9 August 2014), p. 55.
5. The Jönköping healthcare organization is described in Michael Maccoby, Clifford Norman, C. Jane Norman, and Richard Margolies, in *Transforming Healthcare Organizations Leadership: A Systems Guide to Improve Patient Care, Decrease Costs, and Improve Population Health* (San Francisco, CA: Jossey Bass, 2013), pp. 197–218.
6. Morley Winograd and Michael Hais, "How Millenials Could Upend Wall Street and Corporate America," Brookings Institute, Washington, DC (2014), p. 6, at: <http://www.brookings.edu/research/papers/2014/05/millenials-upend-wall-street-corporate-america-winograd-hais> (accessed November 2014).
7. Morley Winograd and Michael Hais, "How Millenials Could Upend Wall Street and Corporate America," Brookings Institute, Washington, DC (2014), p. 9, at: <http://www.brookings.edu/research/papers/2014/05/millenials-upend-wall-street-corporate-america-winograd-hais> (accessed November 2014).

APPENDIX

Developing Strategic Intelligence for Leading Change

If you have answered the questions at the end of the chapters, you have begun to develop strategic intelligence. It's rare that individuals can develop all the qualities of strategic intelligence. However, a team that's leading change is better able to develop these qualities. For each member, developing strategic intelligence starts with what Carol S. Dweck terms a *growth mindset*.[1] This includes making an effort to develop oneself with attitudes of embracing challenges, persisting in the face of obstacles, and learning from criticism and from the success of others. Developing strategic intelligence also requires a *systems-thinking mindset*, starting with a focus on purpose—yours and the organization's. With a systems-thinking mindset, you view organizations and individuals holistically and question how parts and actions interact to further the system's purpose. With this mindset, you ask how the organizational system is adapting to a larger system. In so doing, you will be more likely to gain foresight and openness to the need for change. When the growth and systems-thinking mindsets strengthen each other, you will gain the capability for double-loop learning, the attitude of testing theories with openness to changing those that do not predict expected results.

With these mindsets, you can focus on developing the elements of strategic intelligence. It helps to do this with others. That way, you can see differences in the strengths of each other. In workshops on leadership and strategic intelligence, I have given participants the Strategic Intelligence Inventory (see Table A.1) to diagnose their strengths and the qualities they want to develop. When this exercise is done together with teammates, they can coach each other. They can also compare how they score themselves with how others score them. It may help to have an experienced facilitator to aid in these exercises.

Exercise A.1 Strategic Intelligence Inventory

Score yourself from 1 (low) to 5 (high) on the Strategic Intelligence Inventory (Table A.1).

1. What areas of your strategic intelligence show strength?
2. What areas most need developing?
3. What can you do to improve your personal strategic intelligence?
4. Invite some of your colleagues to partner with you in the spirit of joint learning and development.

Summarize and discuss the differences.

When you give yourself a score between 1 (low) and 5 (high), note the evidence for your score and if it is low, what you plan to do to improve it. If you are doing this exercise with your leadership team, you should display the results of the inventory so that everyone can learn about the team's strengths and challenges.

Table A.1. Strategic Intelligence Inventory

Foresight		
1	I scan the business or professional environment for trends that present threats to and opportunities for my organization.	1 2 3 4 5
2	I seek out and listen to people whose knowledge helps me foresee future trends.	1 2 3 4 5
3	I construct scenarios of possible futures and think about how I would deal with each scenario.	1 2 3 4 5
4	I talk to customers and suppliers about their needs.	1 2 3 4 5
5	I study organizations that are very successful and unsuccessful.	1 2 3 4 5
6	I look for patterns in my business environment that indicate future trends.	1 2 3 4 5
7	I keep track of leading indicators from employees and customers that suggest future trends.	1 2 3 4 5
8	I look for talented people who can become future leaders.	1 2 3 4 5
9	I study unexpected results, consider their implications and opportunities for the future, and act accordingly.	1 2 3 4 5

Visioning		
1	I can describe how my vision uniquely positions my company in the market.	1 2 3 4 5
2	I can describe how my vision takes account of threats and opportunities for the organization.	1 2 3 4 5
3	I can describe my vision as an idealized design of a social system.	1 2 3 4 5
4	My vision for the organization includes how people will interact with one another.	1 2 3 4 5
5	My vision for the organization includes the practical values essential to its implementation.	1 2 3 4 5
6	I can describe the competencies we need to implement the vision.	1 2 3 4 5
7	My vision includes the design and redesign of processes essential to achieving it.	1 2 3 4 5
8	I incorporate the best ideas of my partners in developing the organizational vision.	1 2 3 4 5
9	My vision includes a plan for its implementation.	1 2 3 4 5

Systems Thinking		
1	I evaluate parts of the organization on how well they further the purpose of the system.	1 2 3 4 5
2	I manage the interactions among different parts of the organization.	1 2 3 4 5
3	When I have a problem, I look for contributing factors before I try to solve it.	1 2 3 4 5
4	When I have several things to do, I try to understand how each action will affect the short- and long-term consequences for the system before I act.	1 2 3 4 5
5	When my theories don't work, I question my assumptions about my understanding of the interdependencies within the system.	1 2 3 4 5
6	I make sure we are developing and hiring people with the competence and values essential to achieve the purpose and vision of the system.	1 2 3 4 5
7	I advocate values that further the purpose of the system I lead.	1 2 3 4 5
8	I make sure incentives and rewards strengthen the organizational values and purpose of the system.	1 2 3 4 5
9	I think of my own well-being as an interaction of my physical, mental, and spiritual selves and I work on all three.	1 2 3 4 5

Engaging and Motivating		
1	I communicate a philosophy that people in my organization find meaningful.	1 2 3 4 5
2	I affirm people's strengths and offer them roles that engage their intrinsic motivation.	1 2 3 4 5

3	I do not punish honest mistakes but use them as an opportunity for learning, so that people are not afraid to be open.	1 2 3 4 5
4	I use opposition to reach better solutions.	1 2 3 4 5
5	I understand the motivating values of the employees who are essential to my organization.	1 2 3 4 5
6	I make sure that our processes and incentives strengthen collaboration.	1 2 3 4 5
7	I can tell when people are paying only lip service to the vision.	1 2 3 4 5
8	I make sure people's contributions are recognized.	1 2 3 4 5
9	People in my organization are empowered to propose improvements.	1 2 3 4 5

Partnering

1	I know my strengths and seek out partners who complement my strengths.	1 2 3 4 5
2	I know my weaknesses and seek out partners who can help me develop or can compensate for my weaknesses.	1 2 3 4 5
3	I make sure that my partners in the organization share my philosophy of leadership.	1 2 3 4 5
4	I spell out what I expect from partnering.	1 2 3 4 5
5	I break off ineffective partnering relationships in a timely way.	1 2 3 4 5
6	I partner with key customers to reduce total costs in our joint systems.	1 2 3 4 5
7	I partner with key suppliers to reduce total costs in our joint systems.	1 2 3 4 5
8	I build trust with partners by making sure our philosophies are compatible.	1 2 3 4 5
9	I make sure that my partners will also benefit from our partnerships; relationships are win–win.	1 2 3 4 5

Understanding Yourself and Others

Understanding others starts with understanding yourself. Based on the theories of Freud and Fromm, I developed The Leadership Personality Survey in 2003 and for the past ten years I have given it to hundreds of leaders in workshops and participants in the HEC-Oxford program, Consulting and Coaching for Change. It is reproduced in Table A.2 with a scoring guide and description of the most common types.

Table A.2. Maccoby Leadership Personality Survey

How well does this describe you?	Never	Almost never	Seldom	Sometimes	Frequently	Almost always
1	I want my work to further my own development.	0	1	3	6	10	15
2	I try to develop a vision for the ideal future of the institution.	0	1	3	6	10	15
3	I am an idealistic person.	0	1	3	6	10	15
4	I am satisfied at work if my job allows a great deal of autonomy.	0	1	3	6	10	15
5	I follow the rule that practice makes excellence.	0	1	3	6	10	15
6	I adapt easily to people I like.	0	1	3	6	10	15
7	I've developed my own view about what is right and wrong.	0	1	3	6	10	15
8	I see myself as a free agent.	0	1	3	6	10	15
9	I make my bosses into colleagues.	0	1	3	6	10	15
10	I adapt myself to continual change.	0	1	3	6	10	15
11	I feel I should take the initiative more.	0	1	3	6	10	15

(Continued)

Table A.2. Continued

	How well does this describe you?	Never	Almost never	Seldom	Sometimes	Frequently	Almost always
12	Whatever my job, I try to provide high-quality work.	0	1	3	6	10	15
13	I try to keep my skills marketable.	0	1	3	6	10	15
14	I have a lot of aggressive energy I need to direct.	0	1	3	6	10	15
15	I keep my views to myself because I want to avoid an argument.	0	1	3	6	10	15
16	I put so much energy into responding to others that I feel I lose my sense of self.	0	1	3	6	10	15
17	The best boss for me is a good facilitator.	0	1	3	6	10	15
18	I try to be tough so I won't seem too soft.	0	1	3	6	10	15
19	I am bothered when there is a lack of neatness.	0	1	3	6	10	15
20	I find that the market gives me feedback on my value.	0	1	3	6	10	15
21	I have conversations with myself to clarify what I should do.	0	1	3	6	10	15
22	The best boss for me is like a good father who recognizes my achievements.	0	1	3	6	10	15
23	I want to feel appreciated.	0	1	3	6	10	15
24	I try to keep my options open.	0	1	3	6	10	15
25	I compare myself to highly successful people.	0	1	3	6	10	15
26	I like to collect things.	0	1	3	6	10	15
27	I believe the best decision will result from consensus.	0	1	3	6	10	15
28	I would rather be loved than admired.	0	1	3	6	10	15
29	I like to feel needed by people I care about.	0	1	3	6	10	15
30	What I like about games is the challenge to improve my personal score.	0	1	3	6	10	15
31	I admire creative geniuses.	0	1	3	6	10	15
32	I have difficulty completing projects on time because I want my work to be perfect.	0	1	3	6	10	15
33	Loyalty does not get in my way of doing what is best to succeed.	0	1	3	6	10	15
34	I feel alone and isolated.	0	1	3	6	10	15
35	I am thorough rather than quick.	0	1	3	6	10	15
36	I don't give in when I feel I am in the right.	0	1	3	6	10	15
37	I trust people.	0	1	3	6	10	15
38	I use organizations as instruments to achieve my goals.	0	1	3	6	10	15
39	I keep up with the latest trends.	0	1	3	6	10	15
40	I follow my ideas despite what people say.	0	1	3	6	10	15
41	My sense of security comes from supportive family and friends.	0	1	3	6	10	15

42	I judge people according to strict moral standards.	0	1	3	6	10	15
43	Before I accept an idea, I check it out with people I respect.	0	1	3	6	10	15
44	The best boss for me makes the work group into a kind of family.	0	1	3	6	10	15
45	I feel that I get taken in by people I've trusted.	0	1	3	6	10	15
46	I like to help people.	0	1	3	6	10	15
47	I define quality in terms of what experts value.	0	1	3	6	10	15
48	I don't act until I have fully weighed up the alternatives.	0	1	3	6	10	15
49	I evaluate behavior in terms of what is considered appropriate by the people I respect.	0	1	3	6	10	15
50	I create meaning for myself and for others at work.	0	1	3	6	10	15
51	I am building a network of others who share my values.	0	1	3	6	10	15
52	I enjoy loving more than being loved.	0	1	3	6	10	15
53	I enjoy being part of a cooperative group.	0	1	3	6	10	15
54	I feel better when I save rather than spend.	0	1	3	6	10	15
55	I would rather be admired than liked.	0	1	3	6	10	15
56	I am very tolerant about what others do.	0	1	3	6	10	15
57	I like bringing people together.	0	1	3	6	10	15
58	I sense when people are working against me.	0	1	3	6	10	15
59	I spend a lot of time on details.	0	1	3	6	10	15
60	I like to associate with the top people.	0	1	3	6	10	15
61	I spend a lot of time chatting with my friends.	0	1	3	6	10	15
62	My creativity depends on maintaining my freedom.	0	1	3	6	10	15
63	I enjoy interactions where I can learn something new.	0	1	3	6	10	15
64	I feel I give in too much.	0	1	3	6	10	15
65	Once I start talking I tend to go on.	0	1	3	6	10	15
66	I approach my work as a means to a self-fulfilling life.	0	1	3	6	10	15
67	I try to know everything about everything that impacts my institution.	0	1	3	6	10	15
68	I like to have a schedule and keep to it.	0	1	3	6	10	15
69	The best thing about playing games is having a good time with my friends.	0	1	3	6	10	15
70	I seek out people who can contribute to my plans.	0	1	3	6	10	15
71	I test out my ideas systematically.	0	1	3	6	10	15

(Continued)

Table A.2. Continued

How well does this describe you?	Never	Almost never	Seldom	Sometimes	Frequently	Almost always
72 To be successful, I try to look good.	0	1	3	6	10	15
73 People at work are either with me or against me.	0	1	3	6	10	15
74 I like to keep up with old friends.	0	1	3	6	10	15
75 I rely on certain people who care about me.	0	1	3	6	10	15
76 I put my own spirit into my products and creations.	0	1	3	6	10	15
77 My sense of security is based on my reputation in my field.	0	1	3	6	10	15
78 My self-esteem depends on being seen as successful.	0	1	3	6	10	15
79 I like to develop ways to improve efficiency.	0	1	3	6	10	15
80 I admire people who have helped those in need.	0	1	3	6	10	15

Note that the scoring is an ordinal, not a rational scale. I have increased the scoring intervals to emphasize the differences among people, adding weight to stronger affiliations.

Table A.3 contains the key to scoring the Leadership Personality questionnaire. Write your answer (numerical score) to each question here:

Interpreting the Maccoby Leadership Personality Survey

Table A.3. Scoring chart for Personality Survey

1		2		3		4	
8	____	7	____	6	____	5	____
10	____	9	____	11	____	12	____
13	____	14	____	15	____	19	____
16	____	21	____	18	____	22	____
17	____	25	____	23	____	26	____
20	____	31	____	28	____	30	____
24	____	34	____	29	____	32	____
27	____	38	____	37	____	35	____
33	____	40	____	41	____	36	____
39	____	50	____	44	____	42	____
43	____	52	____	45	____	48	____
47	____	55	____	46	____	54	____
49	____	58	____	53	____	59	____
51	____	60	____	57	____	65	____
56	____	62	____	61	____	68	____
63	____	67	____	64	____	71	____
66	____	70	____	69	____	74	____
72	____	73	____	75	____	77	____
78	____	76	____	80	____	79	____
TOTAL:	____		____		____		____
	Adaptive		Visionary		Caring		Exacting

Leadership Personality

The personalities of leaders color their relationships and influence their strategic decisions and behaviors. Personality focuses the leader's attention on aspects of the future, and may also narrow that focus. Personality influences the types of visions that are meaningful to leaders and the way they think about organizational systems. Their personalities influence the types of people they consider as partners in accomplishing their visions—and the way they recruit, motivate, and empower them.

The Maccoby Leadership Personality Survey provides insight into the way a leader's personality interacts with an organization and the larger society. It is a survey—meaning that it is wide ranging, a full consideration of the aspects of personality affecting leadership. Just as a survey of land has as one of its goals the creation of a map to make the landscape more understandable, the Maccoby Leadership Personality Survey generates a diagram to assist in making the leader's personality more understandable. Only when we understand our personalities are we able to improve them, to become more productive.

You can map your questionnaire scores on this diamond (see Figure A.1).

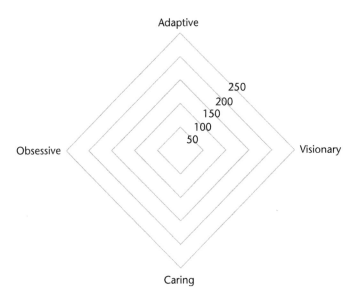

Figure A.1. Graph for personality type questionnaire

Your highest score is your dominant type, the next highest your secondary type. Keep in mind that each person is unique. However, the types are patterns of our value drives or motivational values. You can use the results as a frame for understanding yourself and others.

The personality of every person—and therefore every leader—is a combination or blend of types, which work together as a system. To understand these personality systems, the following pages first present the four types and then consider them in their various combinations with the other types—with an emphasis on leadership.

For some people, a single type is clearly dominant, but never to the total exclusion of elements of the other types. For other people, one type may be dominant and blended with a clear secondary type. Many combinations of the four types are possible.

The Four Primary Leadership Personality Types

1. Caring
2. Visionary
3. Exacting
4. Adaptive[2]

The Caring (Freud's Erotic) Leadership Personality
The most important value of the caring type (see Figure A.2) is loving and being loved. Leaders of this type want to help and care for people. They also want to be seen by others as helpers, to be recognized for their good deeds, to be loved and appreciated, more than respected or admired. They want to believe in other people; to have the trust they naturally place in others be rewarded by reciprocal trust and personal loyalty.

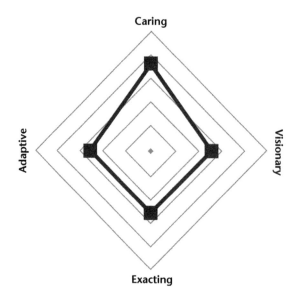

Figure A.2. Graph for caring personality

The caring type dominates the social services, the caring fields—teaching, nursing, social work, mental health and therapy—and service industries, careers that involve nurturing creativity and growth, encouraging others to make more of their lives. They keep our social services running, on both an organizational and personal level, by teaching our children, caring for the elderly, helping displaced, homeless, or poor people, and on a smaller scale, by setting up this friend with that one, lending a hand with moving, or coming over to cook dinner for a sick colleague. They are drawn to organizations that pursue social causes or have social consciences. Yet, they can also be found in sports and the military.

Caring types are typically good listeners; receptive to others and open to hearing about their experiences, ideas, and emotions. They like to share news of personal events and quite naturally expect others to want to do the same.

They never like to say "no" to a favor, thriving on service and cooperation, trusting and relying on friends and family for a sense of security. When caring types rise to leadership positions, it's usually in the caring fields. However, when they are in military leaders, they mentor and forge strong bonds of friendship. They also shine as musicians and performers, who stimulate love in their audiences. However, they can also be found in technical roles as helpers to other leaders. See Table A.4 for a list of strengths and weaknesses of the caring personality.

Table A.4. Strengths and weaknesses—caring personality

Strengths	Weaknesses
• Caring	• Dependency
• Bringing people together	• Gullibility and disillusionment
• Reinforcing social interdependence	• Inability to make tough decisions
	• Fear of taking a stand
• Service and cooperation	• Excesses of emotion
• Trust	• The need for everyone to like them
• Stimulating love	
• Devoted	• Submissive
• Optimistic	• Wishful thinking
• Sensitive	• Easily perceive rejection
• Helpful	• Smothering or intrusive

The Visionary (Freud's Narcissistic) Leadership Personality
The productive leaders of this type (see Figure A.3) impress us as personalities; disrupting the status quo and bringing about change.

Visionaries have very little or no psychic demands that they have to do the right thing. Freed from these internal constraints, they are forced to answer for themselves what is right, to decide what they value, what, in effect, gives them a sense of meaning. The productive ones create their own vision, with a sense of purpose that not only engages them, but may also inspire others to follow them. This vision may be either ethical or unethical, for the common good or for personal power. The visions of unproductive narcissists may be grandiose or irrational, isolating them from others.

Visionaries are accustomed to listening to themselves, their inner voices. They may debate different sides of an issue (e.g. "to be or not to be"), finally reaching a decision about what to do and the best way to do it. They tend to block out the voices of others.

Without the support of others, it's easy to see how visionaries have a highly developed "me- against-the-world" way of looking at things. It often comes out as paranoia, a heightened awareness of danger, which may be realistic, given narcissistic ambition, competitiveness, and unbridled aggressive energy. There's not a lot of gray area in the visionary-narcissistic view of the world—you are either a friend or a foe, for or against the vision, which has become merged with the narcissist's sense of self.

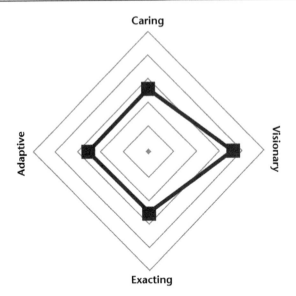

Figure A.3. Graph for visionary personality

Because they have not internalized a strong super-ego in childhood, they are able to be more aggressive than other types.

Productive visionaries are not limited to any particular field; you can find them in almost any field, in any domain. They may not change the entire world (though some certainly have), but they may re-invent their part of the world. See Table A.5 for a list of strengths and weaknesses of the visionary personality.

Table A.5. Strengths and weaknesses—visionary personality

Strengths	Weaknesses
• Visioning to change the world and create meaning that others can share	• Extreme sensitivity to criticism
• Independent thinking/risk taking	• Not listening
• Passionate about ideas	• Paranoia
• Charisma	• Extreme competitiveness
• Voracious learning	• Anger and put-downs
• Persevering	• Exaggeration
• Alert to threats	• Lack of self-knowledge
• Sense of humor	• Isolated
	• Grandiose

The Exacting (Freud's Obsessive) Leadership Personality

Exacting leadership personalities (see Figure A.4) are inner-directed. They live by the rules, and the rules are usually determined by internalized parental figures, forging a strict conscience, or "the way things have always been done around here." People of this type are motivated to live up to the high standards and ideals they set for

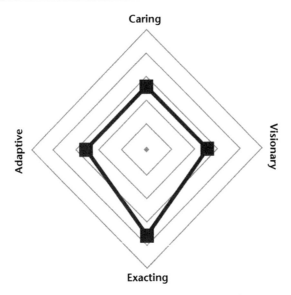

Figure A.4. Graph for exacting personality

themselves, to show, at all times, that they fit the ideal of "good child" to internalized parental figures. When they fail or rebel against these internalized demands, they feel guilty.

They are the conservatives who preserve order and maintain moral values, with a strong work ethic. They focus on the importance of right and wrong, whether at work or in their friendships. Once they believe in someone or something, they stick to it, showing loyalty. They want good, orderly fashion in everything they touch or do, whether it's in their well-kept closets or work space or how they organize their time. The most productive of these types are systematic. They systematically break a task down into its components, and set out to tackle it, one bit at a time.

They are the kind of people who say, "If you're going to do anything, you should do it right." Exacting experts see work as performance, meeting a standard, not necessarily helping anyone. In the past, they were the independent farmers and craftsmen. Today, they are doctors, engineers, financial experts, accountants, scientists, researchers, technicians and craftsmen like electricians, bricklayers and carpenters, as well as the majority of middle managers and some top managers, especially CFOs, COOs, and some CEOs.

An exacting type may make it to the top of a corporation and take on a leadership role, but they are most effective in a company that is itself exacting; a company generally in manufacturing or retail that is conservative, focused on the bottom line, whose success depends on creating processes that improve quality and cut costs, or a government agency. See Table A.6 for a list of strengths and weaknesses of the exacting personality.

Table A.6. Strengths and weaknesses—exacting personality

Strengths	Weaknesses
• Systematic	• Resist anything new or different
• Maintain order and stability	• Get mired in details and rules, lose sight of overall goals
• Preserve tradition	
• Loyal and faithful to their commitments	• More concerned with doing things in the right way than doing the right thing
• Exacting standards, high-quality work	• Control freak, paper-pushing, bean-counting bureaucrat
• Disciplined and diligent	• Judgmental, stubborn
• Determined	• Stingy
• Responsible and accountable	• Extremely neat and clean
	• Always right, know-it-all

The Adaptive (Fromm's Marketing) Leadership Personality

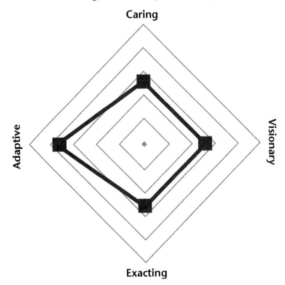

Figure A.5. Graph for adaptive personality

These leaders (see Figure A.5) operate by radar, sensing what the market wants and needs, and then either developing themselves to fit it or just conforming to it. Their self-esteem or self-valuation comes from what could be called a personal stock that goes up and down depending on what they're selling: their accomplishments, how well they align themselves with key people, a client or account base, good looks and style, new skills and expertise, or "whatever," as they are fond of saying. Everything they do is relative; it needs to meet the approval of other people. They rarely use the words right or wrong (as does the exacting type); they want their behavior to be "appropriate." They intuitively know how to adapt to changes in the marketplace, and are not as unsettled by upheaval in the corporate or economic climate as others are. They see change as an opportunity for success and fun.

The most productive adaptive personalities are interactive self-developers. They think of their life and career as continuing education, a chance to pick up new skills, continually learn and grow, intellectually and emotionally. They are the types who want to do well, feel and look good. They exercise, diet, talk to therapists, organize reading and study groups and take classes. They are some of the most productive freelancers, setting their own goals and working well on their own; they are a big part of the current trend towards self-employment, and are excellent at self-promotion. However, they are also natural networkers and team players and enjoy interacting with people like themselves.

This type does well in all manner of sales professions: real estate, public relations, advertising, publicity, events planning, venture capital, money raising. They are effective in consulting, technical design, acting, the arts, publishing, and entertainment. They increasingly play a part in the legal and medical professions because of their ability to bring people together. They are often chosen as school principals and college or university presidents because they make all the different interest groups feel understood and supported; they build coalitions that don't insult anyone. They are the most effective facilitators and the best such leaders, like Bob Iger of Disney, partner with innovative visionaries and exacting operational leaders. See Table A.7 for a list of strengths and weaknesses of the adaptive personality.

Table A.7. Strengths and weaknesses—adaptive personality

Strengths	Weaknesses
• Intuitively adapts to changes in the marketplace	• Indecisive, non-committal
• Superior networking skills	• No center, no inner core that directs them
• Continual reinvention	• No lasting commitment to their work or to people
• Self-marketing	
• Interactive	• Anxiety and uncertainty hang over them, the nagging
• Natural mediator and interpreter between other personalities	question "Is this the appropriate answer? Am I doing OK? Is this working?"
• Tolerant	
• Adaptable	• Indifferent

Combinations of Types

Characteristics of the four personality types are, to some degree, present in every person. Neither the Visionary nor the Adaptive internalize parental commands about right and wrong. But while Adaptives identify with peers and seek consensus about moral decisions, Visionaries determine their own sense of what is right and wrong. A focus on four types is useful as a starting point, but a consideration of the various combinations of types reveals subtleties and the working of the types together as a system to form unique personalities.

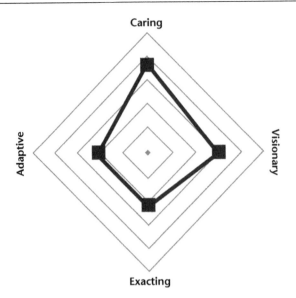

Figure A.6. CARING—visionary personality

CARING—Dominant Mixed-leadership Types
CARING—VISIONARY (HUMANITARIAN)
This type (see Figure A.6) is a humanitarian leader, attuned to the needs of others and ready to take up a social cause or effort for the betterment of others who are in need. They will pour enormous effort into even long-shot chances to help the disadvantaged—often soliciting the help of others in their efforts. Some, like Mother Teresa, begin by caring for individuals in need and then create an order and mission to continue the work.

The unproductive type can let the needs of others drive their business or financial decisions and may give to others to the point that they lose their capacity to give more.

CARING—EXACTING (SEE FIGURE A.7)
The productive leader is the caring but exacting mentor or good counselor, sensing the needs of others, offering advice and helping other people to make their own decisions, or the prototype of the good mother, caring and hardworking and concerned with the health of her children. This combination can be effective as general practitioner doctors and nurses. Some with strategic intelligence have done well as military commanders, such as Ulysses S. Grant and Dwight D. Eisenhower. Caring artists like Wynton Marsalis bring out the best in their collaborators.

The unproductive version is a type that worries obsessively about health issues or about whether they are loved. This type can be too easily manipulated because they fear losing love and can be too trusting.

CARING—ADAPTIVE (SEE FIGURE A.8)
The productive leader is a helper, sensitive and receptive to the needs of many others at one time—or the collective needs of a small group. They excel in situations

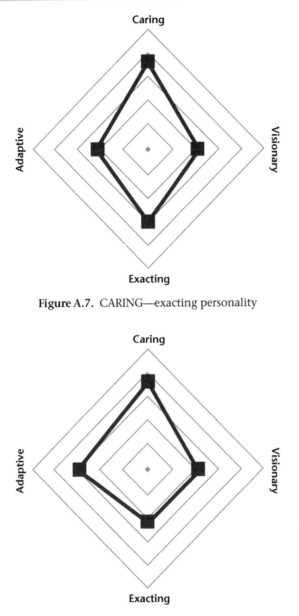

Figure A.7. CARING—exacting personality

Figure A.8. CARING—adaptive personality

where they can support a small group of people or a team. Many psychotherapists are this type.

The unproductive types are constantly looking for a fulfilling relationship. They have many infatuations where they believe they have found themselves, but inevitably decide they have lost themselves.

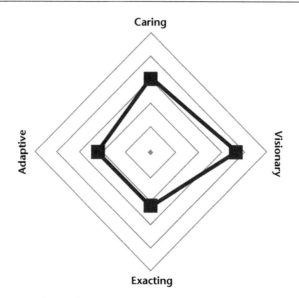

Figure A.9. VISIONARY—caring personality

VISIONARY—Dominant Mixed Leadership Types
VISIONARY—CARING (SEE FIGURE A.9)

The productive version is the institution builder who not only builds an institution, such as a hospital or school, but also leads it and cares for the people, like Father William Wasson (who created Nuestros Pequeños Hermanos, an orphanage in nine countries), creative musicians or actors, like Orson Welles or Marlon Brando. There are also organizational leaders of this type who need to partner with exacting types because they ignore processes and details, focusing on caring for the people who sign on to their vision.

The unproductive version is the Don Juan or Mata Hari type, seductive and exploitative; using the sensitivity to others' needs to find paths open to manipulation and gaining personal power.

VISIONARY—EXACTING (SEE FIGURE A.10)

The productive version is what Freud considered the best strategic leader, combining vision and systematic approaches to implementation. They want results to be accomplished according to a plan, and see the planning process as rehearsal and preparation for action. Jack Welch is a good example of this type. Freud also thought himself this type. Others are Larry Ellison, Steve Jobs, and Jeff Bezos.

The unproductive version is the authoritarian bureaucrat, paranoid, hoarding, and without a creative vision, and lacking interpersonal sensitivity. Rather, the vision is total control and domination.

VISIONARY—ADAPTIVE (SEE FIGURE A.11)

The productive version uses marketing traits in order to recruit others without being controlled by others or trying to please them. Their visions are adapted to people's

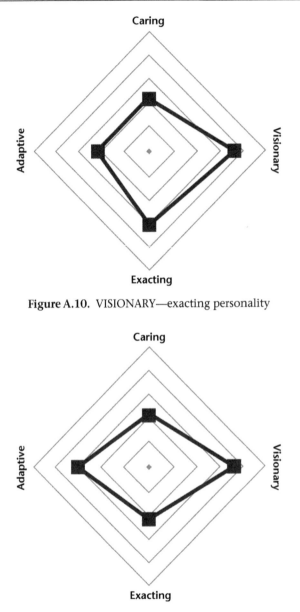

Figure A.10. VISIONARY—exacting personality

Figure A.11. VISIONARY—adaptive personality

needs. Jan Carlzon was this type of leader at Scandinavian Airlines in the 1980s and '90s. Bill Gates and Mark Zuckerberg are other examples. This is the emerging type of the new entrepreneur.

The unproductive individuals tend to suffer from frustrated grandiosity as they continually crank out visions that no one buys, trying to find new and better ways to convince people that their latest project or idea is different than past failed attempts.

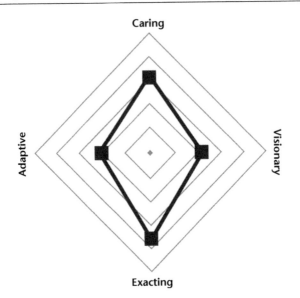

Figure A.12. EXACTING—caring personality

EXACTING—Dominant Mixed Leadership Types
EXACTING—CARING (SEE FIGURE A.12)
The productive leader is the exacting teacher; in business, the person who can identify problems and recommend specific steps to remedy them. They are ideal clinicians and careful doctors. This type is also attracted to professional roles that require people to be systematic and thorough but that want to help people succeed.

The unproductive version is the dependent but rigid type. As bureaucrats, they are servile to bosses but unbending to clients and subordinates.

EXACTING—VISIONARY (SEE FIGURE A.13)
The productive version is the process creator; the leader who can create structure and order in systems that seem otherwise unmanageable. These types believe that making the organization run more efficiently is a great vision. It is likely that they are conscientiously attempting to improve the organization, but not to change the world.

The unproductive version becomes a controlling micro-manager, insisting on compliance with processes and rules that do not contribute to meaningful outcomes.

EXACTING—ADAPTIVE (SEE FIGURE A.14)
The productive leader is the technical consultant, with an emphasis on what they have to offer rather than what others need from them. They focus on developing their skills and looking good, adapting to the market in order to succeed. They are careful to walk the walk, talk the talk, and be informed on all the latest trends that may have an effect on their jobs or their customers.

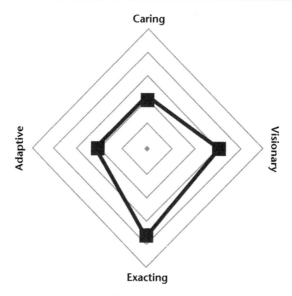

Figure A.13. EXACTING—visionary personality

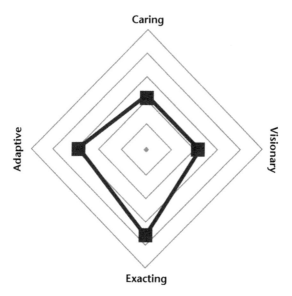

Figure A.14. EXACTING—adaptive personality

The unproductive version is the proverbial "solution in search of a problem." They are so eager to apply their knowledge and expertise that every situation seems to fit in exactly with what they know.

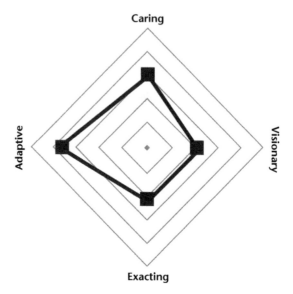

Figure A.15. EXACTING—caring personality

ADAPTIVE—Dominant Mixed Leadership Types
ADAPTIVE—CARING (SEE FIGURE A.15)
The productive leader is the consensus builder. Because they value the needs of many people at the same time, they naturally try to get people to see things from each other's viewpoint. They focus on finding and creating areas of agreement, while gaining some economic and social advantage from helping others. This type is particularly good at sales and public relations.

The unproductive version believes that if they look right and give others what they seem to want they will be loved. They may run into trouble by agreeing with too many people and leaving the impression that they do not have an opinion or standard of their own. They are the perpetual consumers, who believe that they will find satisfaction through buying or experiencing what is fashionable.

ADAPTIVE—VISIONARY (SEE FIGURE A.16)
The productive leader is the guru who is quick to assess the situation and package a customized solution. Because they value both speed and novelty, they are often among the early adopters of new technology, but they can tire of it quickly. In marketing or public relations, they can be the extremely innovative ones who create the perception of new needs in the market.

The unproductive version is unsure of their ideas, continually looking to others to affirm them. They may also suffer from multi-tasking, over-commitment to multiple visions or projects, or from continually changing visions.

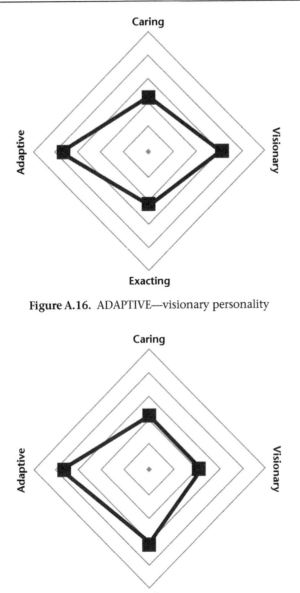

Figure A.16. ADAPTIVE—visionary personality

Figure A.17. ADAPTIVE—exacting personality

ADAPTIVE—EXACTING (SEE FIGURE A.17)

The productive version is especially effective as a technical salesperson or leader of a technical organization or team. Professionals of this type are able to build useful networks and provide value for their clients because they listen well to problems and are systematic in following through. They keep up on the latest information and make good use of it.

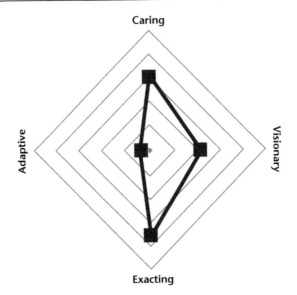

Figure A.18. Farming-craft social character

The unproductive version can be obsessive about getting more information than they can use. They compulsively surf the Internet or wade thought the latest books, magazines, and newspapers in search of the "new."

Mixed Type and Social Character
Personality types are best understood in the context of social character. The socialization process and relationship to the dominant means of production in a society have a significant influence on the meaning that people create for themselves and their value drives. For that reason, the same type will mean something different in each social character.

Farming-craft Social Character
The prototype of the Farming-craft social character is exacting-dominant with a secondary caring (see Figure A.18). Fromm and Maccoby did not find any adaptive types in their study of Mexican villagers. The visionaries were the entrepreneurs who were changing the culture. The productive version of this type is the traditional self-sufficient local producer of agricultural or material goods. In the Farming-craft social character, the dominant personality types tend to be expressed as follows:

Caring—love is directed to family members or apprentices.
Visionary—entrepreneurs starting new business and investing in new technology.
Exacting—in traditional work, done independently, or in the case of farming, with help from family members.

174

Bureaucratic Social Character

In the Bureaucratic social character, the prototype personality is similar to the Farming-craft, but with a little more strength of the visionary and the emergence of the adaptive (see Figure A.19). This type is related to a means of production with strong organizational roles and rules. Production is typically either formatted manual work or more abstract office work; using words and symbols rather than the hand tools of the Farming-craft mode of production.

In the Bureaucratic social character, the dominant personality types tend to be expressed as follows:

Caring—a mentor or a helper to authorities; their caring includes loyalty to organizations or persons they feel are loyal to them.

Visionary—introducing innovative or disruptive ideas within bureaucratic structures; creation of new organizations to seize and control new markets.

Exacting—creation and adherence to structure and process; organization of workflows and systems in linear or hierarchical manners; becoming an expert to gain status and power in the bureaucracy.

Adaptive—first to respond to the visionaries; seeking networks for support.

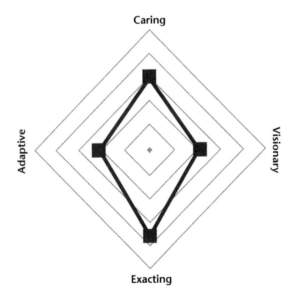

Figure A.19. Bureaucratic social character

Interactive Social Character

The prototype of the Interactive social character is adaptive-dominant, followed by Exacting, Caring and Visionary (see Figure A.20). The moderately productive version of this type is the average personality in the knowledge-service age. They smoothly fit right into the team-based organization of modern knowledge work.

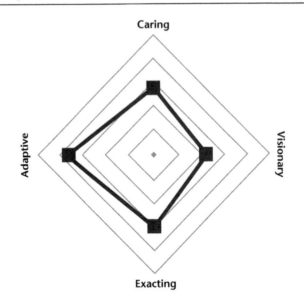

Figure A.20. Interactive social character

In the Interactive social character, the dominant personality types tend to be expressed as follows:

Caring—focused on a person or group; easily directed away to a new person or group that promises greater gain or enjoyment.

Visionary—the "change-the-world" mentality; dissatisfied with the status quo and a desire to recruit people to their change efforts.

Exacting—solving problems or selling services; creating holistic systems that adapt to business needs and make information available across functions.

Adaptive—sensing shifts in market forces and trends, networking, forming and reforming groups to do project-based work; seeking new ways to add value; looking for ways to increase their own marketability.

Your Leadership Personality

> **Box A.1**
>
> Describe, in your own words, your leadership personality: _____
> _____
> _____
>
> Now ask yourself:
>
> 1. What is my leadership type and how does that help me understand the way I lead?
> 2. What type of leadership role best fits my type of leadership: strategic, operational, networking?
> 3. What are my strengths as a leader? What do I need to develop? How do the answers to these questions clarify my responses to the Strategic Intelligence Inventory?

Developing a Leadership Philosophy
Chapter 4 presents the elements of a leadership philosophy. Now that you have read the other chapters, you can see how a leadership philosophy influences visioning and motivating. You should also be able to compare your personal philosophy with your leadership philosophy. When they are consistent, your spontaneous actions will be seen as authentic. You build trust when your actions and decisions model both your personal values and the values you have articulated.

Your leadership philosophy should be consistent with your personal philosophy, and you should be in a role in an organization governed by a philosophy that fits well with yours. The following exercise attempts to clarify your philosophy and how it fits with your leadership role.

Exercise A.2: Leadership Role and Philosophy
1. What is your role as a leader?
2. How does your purpose fit the organization's purpose?
3. Compare your values with the values practiced in the organization.
4. What level of moral decision making do you want to operate as a leader? What is the level practiced in your organization? If there is a difference, what can you do about closing the gap?
5. How do you define results for yourself? How are results defined in your organization? Are these definitions inconsistent? If so, what can you do about it?

The Aim of Change—Building a Learning Organization
In reviewing efforts at transforming healthcare bureaucracies into learning organizations, Cliff and Jane Norman and I constructed a guide to evaluate the components of an organization.[3] It is reproduced in Table A.8 as a final tool for leading change. Idealized design should move your organization's score toward a 10 on all the components. To do so you, and your colleagues will need to employ the qualities of strategic intelligence.

Table A.8. Building a learning organization component evaluation

Components	Score = 0	Score = 2	Score = 4	Score = 6	Score = 8	Score = 10
Purpose and practical values	No written statements	Statement exists	Purpose and practical values defined and visible	Communicated and understood by employees	Used to align and guide the business; roles of people are aligned	Fully integrated into the structure
Processes: systems view	Work as a process is not understood	Major processes and products have been documented.	Relationships between processes are documented	Systems thinking is common.	Systems diagrams are used in business; people's roles are linked to the system	Management systems have integrated the systems view
Partnering	No formal partners	Commodity supplier based on specs and RFQ	Preferred suppliers; recognized quality; traditional contractual relationship	Value-added supplier; distinctive competency; traditional contractual relationship	Alliance partnerships with suppliers; joint projects; sharing of knowledge; relationship at start of project	Strategic partnerships/ common vision; mutual success
People	People are viewed as necessary but replaceable in the bureaucratic organization	People are appreciated for skills they bring; training is viewed as an optional expense	Knowledge and skills of people are important to the organization today; training and education are necessary	People are viewed as important to accomplishing the purpose of the system; development is important	People have a defined role that allows them to contribute to the larger system purpose; people take responsibility for their development	People understand how their role serves the larger purpose and their importance to the future of the organization and achieving the vision
Results: system measures	Financial data is viewed periodically	Financial and other operational measures are used	Family of measures is assembled aligned with purpose	Measures are tracked over time; leading indicators are used for prediction of future results	Variation is understood; measures are aligned with individual roles	Measures are integrated into management systems, values, and roles
Information sources: aid to foresight	Information is gathered on ad hoc, reactive basis	System is based on passive information	System is well documented and includes active sources	Information is documented and communicated; industry leading sources are identified	Comprehensive system with analysis/synthesis for decision making are used in planning and communication	Information sources are synthesized to enable foresight and input to vision

Visioning— idealized design of the future	No vision	Vision statement about being best in class	Vision describes ideal results	Vision is communicated and inspires stakeholders	Vision guides behavior, strategy, developing, testing, and implementation of changes	Idealized vision is realized; a new idealized design is created
Planning to achieve the purpose and implement the vision	No formal planning; reactive planning culture	Planning for improvement is done on an informal basis; inactive	A formal, documented process exists for proactive planning	Integrated process identifies objectives, efforts, and resources	All other planning processes are defined and linked within the organization and with partners	Interactive backwards planning of ideal future system
Leading and integrating change	No formal method exists to manage improvements	Improvements recognized as needed and resources assigned	Learning and improvement utilizes charters and PDSAs routinely	A formal method exists with leaders providing formal guidance for individuals and teams; results are tracked over time	The impact of improvements is understood for the system and fits practical values; improvement is linked to planning and other key business activities	Improvement system is integrated in organization and regularly improved; improvement is completely integrated into all aspects of operating and developing the business
Motivating and aligning people	Employees measured on following commands	Use of financial incentives	Supportive management and recognition	Employees empowered with clear objectives	Managers use all five Rs to motivate	The five Rs are aligned with employee skills and values

Notes

1. Carol S. Dweck, *Mindset, The New Psychology of Success* (New York: Ballantine Books, 2006), p. 245.
2. Reliability and Validity: The Maccoby Leadership Personality Survey is comprised of four independent scales, with Cronbach's Alpha for internal consistency as follows (n = 834):

Caring	0.738
Visionary	0.773
Exacting	0.714
Adaptive	0.714

Face validity of the tool has been very high; there is near-universal acceptance by participants of their descriptions of their leadership personality—especially when the tools are properly facilitated and participants have been guided to read not just one of the primary descriptions, but also the mixed-type descriptions. The survey is a self-discovery tool, not a diagnostic instrument. No construct validity tests have been performed. The data represented here was collected from training programs and seminars over several years.

3. Michael Maccoby, Clifford L. Norman, Jane Norman, and Richard Margolies, *Transforming Health Care Leadership: A Systems Guide to Improve Patient Care, Decrease Costs, and Improve Population Health* (San Francisco, CA: Jossey-Bass, 2013).

Author Index

Subject Index